MORE PRAISE FOR
SHOWING UP

"*Showing Up* is a critical a stand up for gender and racial ____ tes a compelling case that men ____ and equality in the workplace, ____ how to' manual for how they can intervene in ways that make them better men. This book is a must-read for corporate leaders and any man who wants to live up to his potential as an ally and a leader who can shift the world—one workplace at a time."

—**Jennifer Siebel Newsom**, filmmaker
and founder of The Representation Project

"As men, we're trained to split ourselves in two: the rational worker in public, the emotional human at home. What a loss—on both sides of the equation. Ray Arata's great gift is that he can help men connect heads and hearts, passion and productivity. Read this book, and let him show you how to be more present at work and in life!"

—**Michael Kimmel**, author of *Angry White Men:
American Masculinity at the End of an Era*

"In a historical moment when men are called to be and must show up as allies, Arata provides a clear roadmap for what that takes. His approach is brutally honest, self-reflective, and direct. *Showing Up* is a must-read for men on this journey, and for all those who want to call men in as true allies."

—**Gary Barker**, PhD, Cofounder and
CEO, Promundo-US

SHOWING UP

SHOWING UP

HOW MEN CAN BECOME
EFFECTIVE ALLIES IN THE WORKPLACE

RAY ARATA

DIVERSION
BOOKS

For more information, email info@diversionbooks.com

Diversion Books
A division of Diversion Publishing Corp.
www.diversionbooks.com

First Diversion Books edition, January 2022
Paperback ISBN: 9781635769111
eBook ISBN: 9781635769104

Cover design by Libby Kingsbury.
Interior design by Neuwirth & Associates

Printed in The United States of America
1 3 5 7 9 10 8 6 4 2

Library of Congress cataloging-in-publication data is available on file

CONTENTS

INTRODUCTION

WHY SHOULD I CARE?

When it comes to gender equality, equal pay, equity, and equal opportunities, a growing number of men are stepping up as allies to support women and often excluded groups. And a large number of men are not. Why is that?

Many people assume men don't care. If men did care, then they'd act differently, right? I'm here to tell you—based on my experience working with men over twenty years—that most men do care.

They care deeply about their families, the women in their life; about being successful, respected, the best they can be as leaders.

But it's also true that most men aren't in touch with the experiences of women and underrepresented people who face significant challenges. This means men don't always know the best ways in which to show they care—in particular, the ways that matter to those around them.

This was my own experience, which caused me to go through life hurting the people I cared for most. I always saw myself as a "good man," yet I was still not being the ally I should have been to those around me. I wasn't in touch with (nor interested in) how others experienced me. I wasn't awake yet. It wasn't until I became aware of my behavior and its impact on others that I was led to ask myself: Is this the kind of man I want to be?

If you're a man reading this, you may relate. If you're not, I'm going to bet you have a man in your life who reminds you of the one I just described. That man was the "old" me.

MY OWN STORY: BECOMING A BETTER MAN

In the winter of 1999, my family had just moved into a newly renovated house in Marin County, California, as the stock market was climbing. The financial services industry, in which I worked, was booming. Everything felt good.

That is, until my wife came to me early one morning to share something. I hadn't been listening to what she had been trying to tell me, she explained. And what she had been trying to tell me was that my behavior and our relationship weren't working for her anymore. At the time, I was so absorbed in my own notions of what it meant to be a man, a husband, and a father that I couldn't hear her. Additionally, I didn't think anything was wrong. From my point of view, I was providing for my family, I wasn't suffering from any addiction, and I was faithful to her. I was grossly unaware of the impact of my behavior on the most important woman in my life—my wife and mother of my children.

Over time, she'd had enough of my seemingly small actions— expecting the house to be clean when I got home (it was her job after all, wasn't it?), saying one thing and doing another (effectively breaking my word), and not centering my attention on what she needed (because it was all about me). I had no clue what it meant to be accountable. My emotional range was limited to anger, expressed through raising my voice and speaking with the same condescension that I'd heard my father use when I was growing up.

Despite numerous attempts on her part to let me know, I missed the cues until she spelled it out bluntly: She didn't love me anymore. She wanted out of our marriage.

Hearing this was beyond painful, and it also pointed to a bigger issue—I didn't have the tools or training to navigate this. No man in my life had ever modeled emotional literacy for me. So, I did what most men do. I stuffed my emotions down deep and tried to pretend everything was okay. But, predictably, that only made it worse. As a last-ditch effort, I attempted to make promises to her, the kinds of things I thought she wanted to hear. I tried to charm my way out, express remorse—all of my old tricks. But there was no talking my way out of it this time. She had decided.

One month after that devastating break-up, my business partner, who was also a close friend, left our company to go to a rival firm. He cleaned out his office in the middle of the night. I imagine that just like me, he lacked the tools to meaningfully confront real issues.

I was left in a state of shock, with much to contend with—a new mortgage to pay and a family to provide for, all predicated on a business that now felt like it was falling apart.

After my business partner left, I reverted to the same pattern I used when my wife left. I stuffed my feelings. I struggled immensely, with no hope that I'd be able to dig myself out. Nearly six months later—after languishing, getting nowhere, and finding myself in an ever-deeper rut—I experienced the first of many blessings that would help turn things around.

My Turning Point

One afternoon, a colleague asked me to come into his office; he accused me of acting out of control and letting emotions get the best of me. You see, there had been a recent incident at work where I'd angrily yelled at someone over the phone. This was not okay, he explained—which I agreed with completely. As I listened, I realized he was giving me the same feedback about my behaviors that my wife had already shared. He described my actions as often coming from a place of entitlement. This was hurtful, but it rang true.

This colleague then offered me the invitation that would change my life. He encouraged me to attend a personal growth weekend put on by the ManKind Project, a global brotherhood of nonprofit charitable organizations that conduct programs for men. I had never heard of it; he gave me few details but was adamant the weekend had changed his life years before. I accepted his offer and signed myself up.

The weekend is akin to a rite of passage—an initiation into healthy manhood. It helped me to debunk outdated norms of masculine behavior I had adopted and emulated, just like most men. During the workshop, I confronted unexamined beliefs about myself that were driving my behaviors and creating havoc in my personal relationships. I experienced healing that I wasn't anticipating. Most importantly, I discovered that I was able to have a conscious relationship with my emotions. Instead of me reacting without control over what I was feeling, I could actually engage with my emotions in a healthy way.

I learned that if I stayed on the path of being awakened, rather than allowing my inner "little boy" to run the show, I could be healthily masculine in all my roles: father, husband, leader, and friend. This was the beginning of a lifelong partnership between my head and my heart.

Inspired by my new awakening, I wanted more of what I had experienced during the men's weekend. I signed up as volunteer staff for future workshops and joined a local men's group to continue the work I had already started. My intention was simply to "stay awake" and develop those new emotional muscles to serve me in my life.

Little did I know what would come of it: Eight years later, I had racked up thousands of hours of staffing and was actually leading those weekend workshops, along with weekly men's groups.

By 2007, I knew that I wanted to live and lead from the heart in all areas of my life, including my career. I left my financial services job and embarked on a completely new phase of leadership coaching and consulting. I started by sharing what I'd learned by writing a book, and from there, people began looking to me for guidance and expertise about how men could do better—be better.

Around that time, I was introduced to a colleague who worked as a diversity and inclusion consultant. She became intrigued by my work with men and encouraged me to attend a Watermark women's leadership event. At that conference, various women shared their stories and frustration about the experience of working inside companies run mostly by men. It wasn't until then that it became clear to me how slow progress toward gender equality was. It jarred me completely.

The Moment

The courtroom at the Gender Equality Challenge was packed, with several hundred people in attendance. The event, hosted by the mayor of San Francisco at city hall, was attended by several TV crews and an audience of about 85 percent women and 15 percent men. As I sat in the back and listened to the speakers, I realized that progress toward equality might occur more quickly if there was a strategy to actually engage men in the process. I wanted to speak up, but a hot sensation came over me. I was too nervous. By the time I summoned the courage to raise my hand a few minutes later, they had stopped taking questions.

As I walked out of the room, a flood of thoughts entered my mind. I recalled stories my mom had told me of her predicament as the second-born child in an Italian family, where the cultural norm was that the first-born son received the rights and privileges—and the daughter didn't. I thought about my new wife, Anna, whom I'd married two years after my divorce. She had shared her own stories about growing up in an Italian family governed by a strong patriarchal influence. I thought about my daughter who was attending Duke University, only a year from graduating with a degree in computer science. Imagining the challenges she was likely to face as a young woman entering the workforce was just the inspiration I needed to take action.

Using Privilege for Good

Upon the realization that I should do something, that I needed to instigate change, it hadn't yet occurred to me that I had privileges—white privilege, male privilege, and economic privilege—that were available to me to use for this purpose.

I thought back to my men's weekend, how we spent time creating a mission statement for ourselves with the intention of committing to something greater than us as individuals.

We'd been invited to imagine a healed world and what gifts we could bring forward to help create it. This exercise prompted me to reframe what kind of man I wanted to be. I decided to commit to helping create a world with more safety and equality. The gift I decided I could offer in contribution was simple: to live, learn, and lead with an open heart.

In addition to leading men's workshops, I had been speaking at major conferences, appearing on panels, and conducting webinars to audiences largely made up of women. But where, I wondered, could more men like me learn how to be . . . well, better men? There were no conferences that focused on men as partners, leaders, and allies to women and people in under-represented groups.

I felt impatience well up inside me. I couldn't simply wait to find a conference doing this work. I needed to create one. I envisioned that this conference—which was only an idea at this point—would focus strategically on the engagement of men in support of women. My own experience recognizing the parallel between my behaviors with my ex-wife and at work showed me that many of the principles I had taught men outside the corporate world would, in fact, apply inside the corporate world. Healthy masculinity, as a leadership imperative, ought to be modeled by senior heads and management. Men needed to see other men walking the walk. I knew this idea would be successful if I could get other like-minded people, especially men, to align with my vision.

Making My Mission a Reality

I took my mission statement to heart, reaching out to several men and women in corporate roles to share my idea. I wanted not only to create a men's leadership conference that included healthy masculinity as a core driver, but to start a movement. I needed their help and also wanted women to attend. I knew that deep within each man is the desire to be his best self in the roles of spouse, parent, leader, and friend.

I also knew that the current roadmap for masculine behavior—what it means to be a man—wasn't working for anyone, men included. Especially in their personal lives. And it didn't seem like a stretch to presume that this outdated roadmap was also behind the challenges inside organizations. I only needed to speak to a handful of people to validate that the Better Man Conference was needed.

The Time's Up and Me Too movements, in addition to putting the spotlight on men's misbehavior, have helped legitimize the importance of bringing men to the conversation about their roles and responsibilities in inclusion.

The message of the Black Lives Matter movement has only reinforced the need further. I'm doing my part in removing the toxicity that we, as men, all perpetuate (in conscious or unconscious ways); my white privilege creates paths that are easier for me to navigate than those of individuals who are subject to white supremacy and structural racism. I've made the decision to use my privilege for good.

Even though my own wake-up calls turned my life upside down, I am a better man as a result of the changes I've made. And I'm thankful that through my work, I can support other men learning how to do the same.

WHY SHOULD I CHANGE NOW?

Telling men what to do and why is not enough. Unfortunately, most men don't have any connection to why they should change, which is absolutely linked to the actions we need to take as men. This is an important crossroads to recognize. Telling men what to do and why is just not enough. Men either aspire to be a respected ally and trusted leader and are willing to do what it takes, or they don't.

My invitation as a way for you to start this journey is to answer the following questions for yourself:

> Do I want to operate from an outdated and toxic playbook of what it means to be a man, to the detriment of myself and others?
> Do I want to be the man who stands by silently while women and traditionally excluded people are

marginalized? Am I aware that my silence communicates my complicity?

> Do I want to be that guy that gives another guy a pass when he speaks down or makes a joke about women or marginalized groups?

> Do I want to try to become a better man alone, in a vacuum, lying to myself about needing support?

> Do I want to be that guy who doesn't seek input from women or other groups about how they would like to be supported, without imposing emotional labor on them for my learning?

If your answers lead to the clarity of wanting to be better as an ally, that's exactly what we're looking for.

The related question here is, "Do I care enough to make this a priority in my already busy life?" Again, we already know that most men do care. But what, exactly, prompts each man into action can be unique. What prompts you?

For some men, the answer is simple: It's the right thing to do and it aligns with their values. This is the moral case. Others think of their mother, sister, wife, daughter, or female colleague. And these very same people may think of their friends and family members who are part of the LGBTQIA+ and BIPOC communities. This is the personal case. There are a few men who have already experienced the positive outcomes of working with women on their teams and see the business benefit of diverse voices. This is the business case. There is one more, the dinosaur case, that is driven by fear. I offer this: Ponder that if you, as a male ally, don't step up your game and lead more inclusively to help advance others, you will become extinct— just like a dinosaur.

If you are a man reading this book, sit and ponder your motivation. Be honest about it. Being inspired into action for any reason is a good thing. When you understand your impetus for change, you are connected to a driving force that will help you realize your intended goal.

Now, the biggest question: How? Let's dive deep into that right now.

A New Way Forward: Heart-Based Leadership

The Ally's Journey, which I'll be guiding you through in this book, is a repeatable and flexible four-step process based on guiding men and women into heart-based leadership. Heart-based leadership, in action, is when leaders fully utilize their skills and humanity to guide their communication, choices, and relationships with others. **Heart-based leadership requires a skill set of emotional literacy, authenticity, accountability, vulnerability, love, and inclusivity—each of which will be woven through the four steps of the Ally's Journey over the course of the book.**

The Ally's Journey is a framework that I co-created and iteratively improved with my partners, Dale Thomas Vaughn and Ed Gurowitz. It includes the teachings and tools to help individuals and organizations alike advance behaviors to support a more inclusive culture. Ultimately, enabling companies to leverage men as part of diversity, equity, and inclusion initiatives makes it possible for everyone to bring their full—and best—self to work.

Why Leading From the Heart Is Essential

Heart-based leadership augments and supports an organization's analytical prowess. Analytical prowess comes from the power of the mind. Following the mind without including the heart gives us a disconnected starting point. Not everyone connects at the head level, so when we lead by it alone, we're not accounting for the emotional impact of our decisions on human beings. In a work environment, people want to experience a sense of belonging. Employees feel included when they are valued, seen, heard, and understood. When this occurs, they have an emotional response that supports their analytical skill set. This requires that we connect at the heart level.

People are often hired because of their technical skills and knowledge. A heart-based leader who utilizes soft skills to empower others will increase their employees' productivity. When leaders forge a partnership between the head and the heart, they are much more likely to find solutions that reach the greatest number of people. Of even more importance is modeling this skill set for other men so that they may see it in action.

When we add heart-based leadership to organizations, we are meeting a need that can thus unlock the effectiveness of the workforce. Heart-based leadership, which is inclusive of our emotions, enables us to invite the best out of our people. Our abilities to empathize, show vulnerability, and be authentic all help foster trust in others. This encourages everyone to bring their contributions forward. When we come from the heart, we bring another aspect of ourselves to the table, and create a more nuanced, authentic type of leadership.

The Four-Step Ally's Journey

To get you familiar with the transformational path that lies ahead, I'm going to briefly outline each step of the Ally's Journey. We'll get into each more deeply later in the book, but for now, I want you to gain an understanding of the exciting process you're going to embark upon.

> ❯ STEP ONE: Acknowledge bias and privilege
>
> This step will help men and those who seek to be allies understand that this is a journey of self-reflection, discovering your gaps (including both biases and privileges), and

confronting what currently drives your behavior. Included in this step are exercises to become aware of our emotions, the emotions of others, and the unhealthy masculine norms that drive behavior. The purpose of this step is to educate—rather than shame—so that those who want to become good allies can make a conscious choice of how to use their privilege for good.

› STEP TWO: Listen with empathy and compassion

This step focuses on listening to people who belong to typically excluded groups. In my work, I have learned that once men become aware of another person's experiences and challenges, they have empathy—which makes them more likely to move into action. This is an important step because while it's essential to have empathy for others, it's also necessary to have empathy for oneself. This requires us to begin to listen to our own emotions, to experience them and not to avoid them.

› STEP THREE: Take responsibility

Once men have a solid understanding of what is driving their words, choices, and actions, we focus on ownership-driven accountability. Accountability is all about taking responsibility for one's language, actions, choices, and consequences, intended or not—especially in terms of how they impact others. A key to inspiring men to change their behavior is to bring about their understanding of the impact of microaggressions, which can be quite significant. Micro-aggressions show up as a statement, action, or incident regarded as an instance of indirect, subtle, or unintentional discrimination against members of a marginalized group such as a racial or ethnic minority. Microaggressions are a way underrepresented people are negatively affected in both social and working environments (often referred to as "death by a thousand cuts").

Taking responsibility helps you recognize these behaviors: manterrupting, manopolizing, mansplaining, and more. But good intentions don't suffice in terms of recognition. I'll be helping men take responsibility for the way in which their behaviors are impacting those around them.

〉 STEP FOUR: Commit to practices and behaviors

This last step is where the rubber meets the road. Men, women, people of underrepresented groups, and organizations all want to cut to the chase and understand what to actually do. In this step, men will get tangible guidance on how to think, talk, and act like a better man. Men will learn how to lead from the heart; use their privilege for good; support diversity, equity, and inclusion initiatives; and encourage other men to do the same. Finally, we'll talk about protocols for organizations on how to successfully engage, educate, and support men toward contributing to lasting cultural change.

That's it. Those four simple steps can change so much. All it takes is a willingness to go through them with an open heart. And here is the reality: Every day I (and you) start over because it's never a one and done effort.

HOW TO GET THE MOST OUT OF THIS BOOK

Stepping onto the path of becoming an ally and inclusive leader is not something to do alone. If you are reading this book, you likely are feeling that you could use some guidance. I am here to help you with just that.

For Men Reading This Book

It's my belief that there is a common driver within all men that has you wanting to be your best. Making the conscious decision to be your best self will go a long way on your journey as an ally.

This book is a guide for looking inward and challenging your current thinking on what it means to be a man, both in the context of being an ally, and a leader or follower. Even more so, this book is intended to help you be more heart-centered—something that hasn't been modeled for most men.

There are several "invitations" for you to consider and absorb. Take the time to read and fully consider the questions I ask throughout our time together. The best way to use this book is to spend some time reflecting on your own masculinity—what you saw modeled for you—and to be honest about where it has not or does not serve you. I encourage you to come to this work with a beginner's mind.

A few pointers to consider:

> Each chapter builds on the prior one, so it is best to read each chapter in the order they are presented. Only proceed to the next chapter when you feel comfortable knowledge-wise in what you just learned.
> Be gentle and kind with yourself. Shame has no place on your journey as an ally. Yes, you have made mistakes and will continue to make mistakes—and that's okay. You are

human. Making sure that you learn from those mistakes is the critical part.

> Seek and be open to feedback. You will only grow if you get the support of others.

> Resolve to stay on the journey. You will be surprised by how women and people who belong to marginalized groups appreciate your commitment to being better. Commit, even if there are missteps on your part.

> Embrace learning opportunities for yourself and others. Apply your learning as soon as possible. Look for opportunities to change your behavior, and that of others, every day.

> Stay humble. It has been my experience that men often feel they are farther along on the path than they really are. Many women and people who belong to underrepresented groups have echoed this to me, about me! Understand that where you are and where you think you are may be totally different—and practice acceptance of that gap. Be comfortable being uncomfortable.

For Women and Members of Typically Marginalized Groups Reading This Book

If you are a woman or a member of a marginalized group, this book can be used to better understand how to relate, engage, and partner with men in the context of healthy masculinity and heart-based leadership. While it's the responsibility of men to better themselves, it is hugely helpful for those that they interact with to understand the process of transformation they are undertaking. It takes all of us to change the narrative and create a better culture in our homes and workplaces.

I have been approached by many who, after attending my talks or experiencing our conferences on heart-based leadership, have a deeper appreciation for the stories of men and the struggles they face in becoming allies. This is not to say that their unreformed behavior was okay; rather, it's helping to create a bridge of awareness toward each other's journey. I will never understand what it feels like to be in any group other than my own. Because so many of you have helped me become more aware of your stories, I can take responsibility to do my part and support others like me to learn as opposed to putting additional emotional labor on you.

For Members of Organizations Reading This Book

If you are a DEI professional, HR professional, Learning and Development professional, a stakeholder, or anyone committed to the culture of your business, this book will help you to understand the various factions of men that exist in your company. I will share with you the impediments and influences that may be currently playing out regarding the men in your organization, so that you can successfully engage them. And I'm going to offer insight in how to support your male leaders by sharing successful ways I talk to and teach men at a personal level.

Many DEI professionals struggle with how to include men in their DEI efforts. There is no easy way, other than to recognize that success requires their engagement (especially because the majority of leadership roles are currently filled by men). You need a top-down approach that enrolls leaders into emulating the behaviors you want to see from all men in your organization.

This book will help make you an ally-in-training and provide a roadmap that organizations can follow to get everyone on staff invested in changing the culture around them.

WHAT YOU CAN EXPECT FROM THIS BOOK

Throughout *Showing Up*, I'm going to:

> Present challenging real-life scenarios, putting you in the shoes of the people in these stories;
> Bring in other experts to lend their subject-matter expertise to what I am teaching, and share important exercises you can practice;
> And end each chapter by summarizing key lessons for your learning that can be used as tools throughout your journey.

CHAPTER ONE

SET TO WIN

The Me Too, Time's Up, and Black Lives Matter movements have created a perfect storm of bad behavior, largely due to men's toxic behavior. These movements were a long overdue response, as well as an outright refusal to tolerate this type of behavior. Men are on high alert: The spotlight is squarely focused on their behaviors, and we have already witnessed a number of "high profile" instances of men being fired, stepping down from leadership, and finding their careers ruined by their choices and behavior, as well as their abuse of power. Their careers were tarnished after social media exposed their actions. These very same men work inside companies and are often in leadership positions, thus posing a question for many organizations: Do we ignore, react, or take initiative? What is your position?

One thing is for sure: The underlying playbook of what it means to be man, and how it shows up in our roles as leaders, partners, spouses, and parents, needs a rewrite. The writing is on the wall. It's time for us individually and collectively to embrace healthy masculinity as a way of being, in our personal and business lives. Not only will those we care about benefit; we will, too. Company cultures that have a predominance of men in leadership are ripe for change. How you change just depends on what will motivate you to change.

Troy Young, president of Hearst Magazines and publisher of *Good Housekeeping*, *Cosmopolitan*, and *Town & Country*, resigned in July 2020 due to allegations of sexual misconduct. For most companies in a situation like this, there isn't a playbook; they have to create one.

The Hearst Corporation is one example of how one man, through his misconduct, can create a **wake-up call moment** for the leadership of a company. How and if a company answers a wake-up call says a lot about them. How you or your company answers says a lot about *you*.

A "wake-up call" is a shock, surprise, or realization that causes you to become fully alert to what is happening in your life. It can also be thought of as a glimpse into a moment of truth, where you see that staying on your current trajectory and not changing only creates more pain. A wake-up call of this magnitude gives a company a snapshot of its culture and creates a choice point for moving forward.

Hearst chose to answer the wake-up call in a healthy masculine way.

iCrossing, a subsidiary of Hearst, hosted the 2018 Better Man Conference in the Hearst Tower in Midtown Manhattan. When this all went down, they reached out to my company to address their culture issue head on. Their resulting commitment was to sponsor and send seventy senior executive male leaders to our fall 2020 virtual Better Man Conference as a kick-off event, to be followed by a training course on allyship with an emphasis on healthy masculinity. The men were eager to learn so that they could do their part and play a role in shifting their work culture.

This is just how one company responded. Organizations have been slow to initiate efforts to engage men as allies and inclusionary leaders until either they see business benefits or their hand is forced. It appears that the tide is changing for organizations, albeit slower than it should.

Some companies are making bold goals that *require* the engagement of men as allies and inclusionary leaders. The Intel Corporation, which has been a partner, client, and sponsor of the Better Man Conference over the years, made one of its goals for 2030 to increase the number of women in technical roles up to 40 percent. This, in essence, would double the number of women and traditionally excluded minorities in senior leadership. They recognize that in order to make this goal a reality, they must include men in their DEI efforts.

The wake-up calls just keep coming. I invite you to consider another wake-up call moment that has presented itself to you and the company you work for: COVID-19 and the Black Lives Matter movement.

LeanIn.org and the consulting company McKinsey conducted a 2020 Women in the Workplace study that looked at the pandemic's impact. According to its results,

Women in particular have been negatively impacted. Women—especially women of color—are more likely to have been laid off or furloughed during the COVID-19 crisis, stalling their careers and jeopardizing their financial security. The pandemic has intensified challenges that women already faced. Working mothers have always worked a "double shift"—a full day of work, followed by hours spent caring for children and doing household labor. Now the supports that made this possible—including school and childcare—have been upended.

In December of 2020, largely due to the pandemic, 100 percent of jobs lost were held by women. In December 2020, women lost a total of 156,000 jobs while men gained 16,000 jobs, according to the National Women's Law Center: "Of the net 9.8 million jobs lost since February 2020, women's jobs have accounted for 55% of them."

As a result of these dynamics, more than one in four women are contemplating what many would have considered unthinkable just six months ago: downshifting their careers or leaving the workforce completely. This is an emergency for corporate America. Companies risk losing women in leadership—future women leaders—and thus unwinding years of painstaking progress toward gender diversity.

This business pain is real for many organizations. Is this happening at your company?

Personally, I seek to find the silver lining in challenging times. Amidst this crisis there is an opportunity. Do you see any silver linings? As a result of COVID-19, are you making adjustments in your leadership?

If organizations prioritize building a more flexible and empathetic workplace, they may be able to retain the employees most affected by today's crises—women—and nurture a culture in which women have equal opportunities to achieve their potential over the long term. Men will need to develop their own ability to be empathic. This includes you!

You might be wondering: How is engaging men as allies and inclusionary leaders good for business? On a more personal note, how is it good for you?

The compelling reason for companies to engage men as allies centers around attracting, retaining, and hiring talent. Creating a culture of belonging wherein men are active allies increases the likelihood that people bring their whole selves to work, which increases overall effectiveness. Unless you have men on board and part of diversity and inclusion efforts, the status quo for men in charge will remain, and the lack of opportunities for those who don't identify as men will slowly erode a company's ability to be competitive.

HOW DO WE GET MEN ON BOARD?

Maybe you are a diversity and inclusion professional or head of a women's employee resource group (ERG). Maybe you have leadership responsibility in your organization and are reading this book for support in your role. I'm going to speak to you in your organizational capacity directly below; I encourage you also to read sections where I directly address the men who are reading this to better understand what's true for them.

Maybe you are an inspired male leader or a man who self-identifies as an ally, or you simply want to be one. Maybe your company bought this book and asked you to read it, or a woman colleague gave it to you. So that you may effectively engage yourself to be part of a culture change, it is imperative that you understand where you fit into the states of men as they currently exist in your company. I will speak to you as an individual.

WEARING THE ORGANIZATIONAL HAT

If you have an organizational responsibility (DEI, HR, Learning and Development), knowing the states of men in your company as well as barriers and impediments that many men face allows you to "walk in their shoes." This ultimately supports how you "meet them where they are."

A question you need to address: What influences the men in your organization and what limits or drives their behaviors? Both organizations and men must know the answer to this question so as to identify and offer the training men need to be allies and inclusionary leaders who support culture change. **There are five areas to examine:** social/political narratives (including racism and white supremacy), COVID-19, men not feeling the pain of others, man box behaviors, and power.

For those of you wearing an organizational hat, read the section below to better understand the states of men in your company.

If you are an individual, read this section to see which state you most identify with.

The States of Men

Over the years, I've heard men self-describe where they were with respect to equality, being an ally, and participating in their company's DEI efforts. I've listened to them share their current experiences, their frustrations, their aspirations, and more. From these anecdotes, I have categorized the states of men inside organizations.

Some men believe that their companies' DEI efforts threaten their jobs.

These men, by virtue of their perception of DEI efforts as a threat, demonstrate how their privilege is invisible to them when they articulate that "their" job is threatened. My friend and colleague Michael Kimmel, an activist and author, says, "Privilege is invisible to those who have it." The key word indicating that point is "*their*"—as in, *their* job. It isn't their job; they don't have a preordained right to it over anyone else.

Organizational Guidance: Supporting these men to understand their own privilege by humanizing it, and to realize that

SET TO WIN ⟨ 7 ⟩

with privilege comes responsibility as well as the opportunity to use it for good, is the approach to take. (Chapter four will explore privilege in great detail, along with exercises to support your learning.)

Some men don't feel included in their companies' DEI efforts.

Many companies have supported the establishment and maintenance of employee resource groups, creating communities inside companies for LGBTQIA+ folks, women, BIPOC (Black, Indigenous, and People of Color), disabled person/people, and neurodivergent people. There are very few companies that support or have ERGs for men. As a result, men who want to be part of a company's diversity efforts can join other ERGs and begin to learn about becoming an ally, but what this scenario doesn't do is center whiteness, nor does it create a sense of community for men. As a result, it doesn't fulfill men's desire to be more involved.

Organizational Guidance: Providing men with training that supports allyship, and encouraging men to start an ERG, is another option. This will be covered later in the book.

Lots of men are afraid to say or do the wrong thing, so they say and do nothing.

This is largely how many men feel currently. They are the bystanders. They are complicit.

Organizational Guidance: These men need training, as well as other leaders inside their own organizations, to be models of allyship and inclusion. This will be covered later in the book.

Some men want to be part of the solution but don't know what to do or say.

These are the men you want to activate and build with.

Organizational Guidance: These men need training and can be used to build momentum inside companies to legitimize allyship training. I often suggest that DEI professionals focus on this group of men first. They are eager and are usually willing to bring along other men.

A few select men are already acting like allies and already understand. These men are the ones who get it. They don't need training because they already act like allies and inclusionary leaders. These guys attend other ERG events, often sponsor events in an executive capacity, and sometimes mentor women.

Organizational Guidance: Where these guys are needed is in the strategy of enrolling other men. I encourage companies that are considering training or participating in the Better Man Conference to "stand up" these types of leaders in front of their workforce, supporting training efforts with the idea that other men will see, respect, and follow these men.

《　》

Knowing these factions of men is helpful. Behavioral change requires a deeper look and an understanding of what is currently driving men's behavior.

AREAS WORTH YOUR ATTENTION

The numerous influences that impact men are detailed below. For those in an organizational capacity, consider this section a broad overview. For the men reading this, consider this an opportunity to take a personal and honest inventory of yourself. I will speak specifically in each section with a question or two for you to consider.

Understanding the Impact
of the Current Social and Political Narrative

Start by examining the optics for most men—where their levels of cognizance and curiosity and willingness to address their own behavior are at—with respect to the current social and political narrative. This includes racism and sexism.

Empowered by social media and its immediate transparency in support of these movements, employees are demanding cultures of inclusion with opportunity for all. Any missteps by men or the organizations they work for are immediately spotlighted.

This has been a necessary and unfortunate part of the narrative that has also left, in its wake, many men unsure of how to act or deal with past transgressions. Lacking a clear path to healing on their way to being a better man and leader, many men function as bystanders and stay silent.

There will always be the few bad apples, and until more men stand up and put themselves on the path of being allies, the inaction of the majority is what we need to focus on. That inaction is part of the problem, not just the actions of the few. Tony Porter, founder of A Call to Men, puts it best when he asks: "Why is it that we, as men, allow the 'few' to control the overall narrative of men? Why can't we, as men, collectively and in unison rewrite the narrative and do away with violence, abuse, and the lack of equality when it comes to women?"

Even those who are willing to take accountability for past actions before being spotlighted, in their efforts to be a better man, pay big prices for coming forward, but not nearly as big as the price paid by those who are harmed.

From Super Size Me to Downsize Me

I had the opportunity to meet Morgan Spurlock, director of the award-winning documentary *Super Size Me*, when I was in

New York for the Better Man Conference in 2018. I had been introduced to him by a male colleague who had shared with me that Morgan was looking for some guidance on how to move forward as a better man. He was ready to take accountability for his past behaviors.

Morgan had shared with me, and also publicly, that he had a moment of clarity/crisis of confidence. Without thinking about it, he wrote a blog post admitting sexual misconduct in his past, including cheating on his past wives as well as settling a sexual harassment allegation.

For Morgan, the consequences were severe. His production company went from sixty-five people to less than five in a matter of weeks; his second documentary following *Super Size Me* was pulled. Despite this, he maintained a good attitude and was determined to move forward.

I share this story to highlight that taking accountability for one's past transgressions is the road less traveled, and with it comes consequences that few men are willing to take on. Morgan took the risk, paid a price, and most importantly, he sought a path to learn and be better.

In no way am I condoning his behaviors; I'm simply illustrating that most men choose to stay silent for fear of annihilation rather than take accountability and face consequences. This has to change, or we will never progress from where we are today.

Countless stories in the media reinforce the lack of a middle ground. There needs to be some path of healing; that path has yet to be illuminated. While this story may not resonate personally, I invite you to examine for yourself: What risks are you willing to take to be an ally, despite your past?

Men: Maybe you presently understand that some behaviors in your past likely impacted another person negatively; you might feel bad about something you did and it's important to process.

What's most important to process is that you now have awareness of how your actions may have hurt another person. Notice any emotions that might come up. I will address in a future chapter how to effectively respond to these emotions instead of impulsively reacting—or worse yet, stuffing them down.

At this point, there is only one obvious choice of action: to put yourself on the path of becoming an aware and awake ally in all that you say and do. In the end, it's less about what you did and more about who you choose to be going forward. I am going to assume positive intent on your behalf—that this is why you are reading this book!

Understanding the Impact of COVID-19

With the movements of Time's Up, Me Too, and Black Lives Matter gaining ground, COVID-19 entered the picture and drastically forced the issue of men stepping up at home and work. For a moment, let's look through a heteronormative lens: COVID-19 has spotlighted many areas that traditionally fall on the shoulders of women. Cooking, cleaning, shopping, supervising their children's distance learning while working their own job that may or may not have an understanding boss or manager. It is simply too much for one parent to undertake. If there was ever a time to put aside gendered home responsibilities, it's now, under the new conditions of remote work that COVID-19 largely introduced to our lives. Maybe you have already made adjustments at home; if that's the case, then you are ready to look for opportunities to step up and contribute in the workplace.

I want to acknowledge that COVID-19 has affected everyone's life at home: those in same-gender partnerships, those with and without children, those living alone, and those in limited opportunity families. Regardless, everyone needs to chip in and be supportive.

The pandemic's effect on business and personal life has been to call men forward to re-evaluate outdated and gendered norms of behavior at home and work. The way forward is to recognize that being allies, partners, and leaders is not just good for women, but for men as well.

Getting real in times of crisis

On day one of shelter in place, I was on a video call with my partners. I looked through the screen and saw faces of pain. As a matter of practice, we as partners routinely do a check-in to start our meetings.

A check-in is an opportunity to look inward, check how I'm feeling, acknowledge what's challenging me . . . to get real and to share it with others. This does several things: It allows me to share where I am at by speaking my truth, to be heard and not judged by others, and for others to do the same. This fosters the necessary connection that we need to work well together.

On this twelfth day in March of 2020, each of us had some difficult truths to share. They were heavy truths. An idea and question popped into my head: Why shouldn't leaders in companies have the opportunity to use this technology?

Aren't they going through the same thing we are? I bet command and control is very tempting, that there is a lot of fear present with not much humanity. I wondered if leaders would be interested in participating in a live Zoom call that would provide space for them to get the benefit of what we were regularly experiencing.

I reached out to several men at companies like Oracle, Intel, and Genentech. I shared my idea and I immediately got responses. One of them shared with me that command and control blew up in his face at home: he had cried twice, and would definitely be interested in attending.

Over 125 people showed up to our first call, validating my intuition that more men than ever are ready to step on the path of becoming inclusive leaders and allies. We put people in small breakout rooms and created the space for them to "get real," be introspective, and ground themselves so they could do that with others.

Leader/Organizational Guidance: Leaders can encourage candid conversations because *tending to the business of being human allows people to tend to business.* Organizations can promote a conversation series.

We Don't Feel the Pain

When it comes to equity, belonging, and inclusion, most women and people of marginalized groups would be able to share quite clearly the challenges they routinely face, in their personal lives and work lives, just for being who they are. That is because it is their *lived experience.*

They could illuminate what these challenges cost them, whether it be their personal or professional relationships, job opportunities, financial success, and even their own health and well-being. Women and people of underrepresented groups would likely share that they are tired (exhausted, actually), stressed, resigned, sad, afraid, and angry. To hear and understand that this is their experience is to acknowledge their pain.

Often, white men are unaware of the challenges, frustrations, and the short- and long-term impacts that these individuals face every day of their lives—because it's not *their* lived experience. These same people might well be our friends, work colleagues, family members. Through the optics of a white man, the often-subconscious observation is that "All of this is happening around men but not to men." As for BIPOC men and gay men, this may not be the case.

If we aren't being denied opportunities based on our gender and our identities, or not having to work twice as hard to adhere to a double standard simply because of who we are, then it doesn't get our attention—because it's not happening to us. And this certainly is not an excuse. We're simply not experiencing the pain.

Guidance: One way to get men engaged as allies is to bring to their attention the experiences of people who don't look like them or who are different to evoke some empathy. What follows is an example of an effective training strategy we use inside companies.

Presencing the real-life experiences of others

In my work engaging men as allies and inclusionary leaders, I've witnessed time and time again that when I bring to men's attention (without shame or blame) what is happening to the women they work with—that the women are having an entirely different experience than they are, under the same roof—it often comes as a surprise.

The power of senior leadership vulnerability

In the fall of 2018, my partner and I were hired to deliver a training to the male leaders of a well-known global newsroom. We initiated the process by interviewing three women and three men, to get a pulse of the then-current working environment. Each interview was slated for one hour.

Calls with the men each concluded after twenty minutes. Their perspective of the workplace culture was that the men were open to change for the right reasons; that it was a good, diverse workplace (though things could always be better); and that the environment felt equal and open—merit-based.

Calls with the women went the full hour. What we heard was very different.

We heard:

> ❯ Women are set up to fail—they are given difficult assignments with insufficient support, and if it doesn't work, they're gone. Men in the same situation get support and resources.
>
> ❯ Women need to be perfect to get a shot, and *then* they get training. Men can be less than perfect and get staff and support rather than training.

When we shared our findings with the diversity leaders who hired us, they wanted us *to not include the slide* we had appropriately titled, "The tale of two companies." (That's not what happened.) When you start on your journey, I ask that you allow all the feedback to be listened to. To not allow a form of complicity to take place.

But when we showed the slide to the editor in chief, he insisted on keeping the slide as part of the presentation. In addition, he stood up in front of a room full of mostly men and made clear that this was not the kind of newsroom culture he wanted to see or be part of. He shared that he, too, had things to learn, that he made mistakes, and that he had not been as aware as he would have liked. He pledged to do more and committed to changing his behavior.

When a male leader stands up in front of a room of men, admits his own failings, takes accountability for what happens on his watch, and publicly commits to be better, it's a powerful model to emulate and follow for the men in the room. It also sends the message to the women that men are capable of making the transition to be more inclusive.

Organizational Guidance: Senior leaders must play a very strategic and important role in activating the men inside their organization. Identify that senior male leader who is willing to stand up in front of other men, be vulnerable, own his mistakes, and share his reason for why being an ally and inclusive leader is important to him as well as to the company.

The newsroom's editor in chief took ownership of the work environment that was in place on his watch and made it clear that he would do his part in changing the current culture to be more inclusive.

This is another step in the right direction to get men engaged, but it still falls short of what is required at a personal level for men to "activate" and get on board.

Empathy activated

When he finished, the room was eerily quiet. The looks on men's faces were contrite, surprised, and questioning. We invited them to share their responses to what they heard and many of them said, "I had no idea," "what can I do," "this is not ok with me," and other variations on these three common responses.

For these men, their ability to empathize started with the journey from their heads to their hearts—when they were able to hear and connect to the experiences of others in their own newsroom. We subsequently were hired to bring the same training to their UK office.

Organizational Guidance: Bringing live and tangible experiences of the women in your organization, without shame or blame, makes it real for men. Second, and of equal importance, is to present instances of racism. When men are presented with this information—that their actions and inactions, language, and decisions are behind the experiences of the women and people of color they work with—most men want to be better. This is an experience to build upon.

Outdated Notions of Masculinity and the
Influence of Man Box Behaviors

There exists an unofficial playbook of what it means to be a man, handed down from prior generations. Men before us—our fathers, grandfathers, uncles, brothers, teachers, coaches, and society at large—adapted, accepted, and modeled this playbook.

It's not consciously talked about; it's just always been so, with many people paying the price of unhealthy masculinity.

Women, too, accepted and encouraged these behaviors for a variety of reasons. It was what they saw and experienced, and they didn't feel they had a voice or a choice to reject these unhealthy versions of masculinity.

Times have changed: Women have spoken up and organized themselves, and more and more men want to be on the right side of change, with healthy masculinity leading the way. In order to pave the way for a healthy rewrite of what it means to be a man, we must first understand the man box. Unpacking these drivers is a necessary component that paves the way for healthy masculine leadership.

Understanding the man box and its evolution

Writer and activist Paul Kivel's *Act Like a Man Box* refers to a narrowly defined set of traditional rules for being a man. These rules are enforced through shaming and bullying, as well as promises of rewards, the purpose of which is to force conformity to our dominant culture of masculinity—and to perpetuate the exploitation, domination, and marginalization of women and people who are queer, genderqueer, and transgender.

In the early 1980s, Kivel and others at the Oakland Men's Project gave birth to this powerful central pillar of men's work. They developed *Act Like a Man Box* in their work with adolescents in public schools around the San Francisco Bay Area. In 1992,

Kivel documented their workshop process in his book *Men's Work: How to Stop the Violence That Tears Our Lives Apart*. It was here that Kivel published his *Act Like a Man Box* workshop, graphics, and everything we have come to define around the term.

In the mid-1990s, A Call to Men founder Tony Porter was doing men's work in Rockland County, New York, as well as serving as the director of an alcohol and drug treatment program at Nyack Hospital. At that time, local service organization Volunteer Counseling Services invited Paul Kivel to speak. Porter states it was then that he first heard the phrase "act like a man box."

Over time, Porter, who was working with populations of men in penitentiaries and other challenging spaces, determined that the "Act Like a Man Box" language would not work with these populations. In 2010, Porter recorded his TED Talk titled "A Call to Men," which to date has been viewed over 2,600,000 times on the TED site alone. Porter drove the man box into global public awareness and made Kivel's pioneering work into a household term.

In 2019, I invited Tony Porter and Mark Greene, former senior contributing editor to the Good Men Project and author of *The Little #MeToo Book for Men*, to present at the Better Man Conference in New York City (hosted by Moody's). These man box behaviors were running rampant in corporate cultures, and many of them were negatively influencing leadership behaviors. The audience loved the material, and we have incorporated it into our workshops.

What are some of these unwritten, yet subscribed to, rules?

1. Real men don't show their emotions, but anger is okay.
2. Real men are always confident. (We won't show you our insecurities or admit we don't know.)
3. Real men don't ask for help.
4. Real men make all the decisions.
5. Real men are providers, not caregivers.

6. Real men are heterosexual and sexually dominant.
7. Real men continuously talk and play sports.
8. Real men are never handicapped, disabled, or unemployed.

Mark Greene has said, "Men and women deserve better than a masculine culture of dominance which churns out broken men." He's right. Maintaining the idea of stoicism over emotionality is, without question, the most hurtful result of the man box. When men seeking to be allies and inclusionary leaders don't express themselves emotionally, not only does it discourage others from being authentically human, it also severely limits their capacity for creating authentic relationships, leading effectively, and more.

Power: The Elephant in the Room

In addition to the aforementioned impediments that leave men reluctant to engage as allies and leaders, there is another potential reason for their reluctance: power. Men are accustomed to the power that comes with leadership. Giving up that power, or even simply the idea of giving it up, may give men pause. For some men, the idea of sharing leadership and thus affording others access to leadership positions is a perceived loss of power.

Why not come at it from a different angle? Power can be used to include, as opposed to exclude. Power can be used to support and advance others. Let's shift the zero-sum thinking of "if you win, I must lose," to "we both can win."

The impact of the Black Lives Matter movement

With senseless killings of Black people by police occurring around the country, and 2020's summer of activism in response, the topic of racism (that was always there and now can't be ignored) has made its way into corporate America's leadership ranks and board rooms—and it isn't leaving anytime soon. These experiences are painful; if there is to be healing and inclusivity inside companies, male leaders must learn to apply the same techniques taught in this book to combat not only sexism but racism, as well.

A QUICK LOOK BACK

The current wake-up call companies and men are hearing in the workplace is the demand for behavioral changes that can, and will, positively affect cultures of inclusion. There is a lot at stake for companies to consider: the effect of COVID-19 on women in their organizations, the hiring and retaining of people who belong to marginalized groups, and the growing need to engage more men in diversity and inclusion efforts. Additionally, the Black Lives Matter movement has rightfully led companies to address racism along with sexism.

To understand how organizations can effectively engage men as allies and inclusive leaders, we've looked at what men are facing personally as a result of the current social and political narrative, and what challenges COVID-19 and the Black Lives Matter movement have presented. This is just the exterior. We have also illuminated man box rules that currently drive many male behaviors. Just as important is understanding that men don't initially connect to the pain of exclusion unless it's happening to them, which necessitates presencing the pain of others so as to evoke empathy. Finally, we offer a reframe of power from zero-sum thinking to win-win.

Healthy Masculinity as a Feature, Not an Option

With a better understanding of how *unhealthy masculinity* plays out and often interferes with men engaging as allies and inclusionary leaders to support cultures of inclusion, there is an opportunity to "rewrite the playbook" on what it means to be a man in our roles as leaders, fathers, partners, husbands, and colleagues.

While healthy masculinity may vary slightly for each individual, I offer the following for all of us to consider aspiring to. Healthy masculinity might look like:

> ⟩ Men showing, sharing, and experiencing their emotions.
> ⟩ Men admitting to themselves and others that it's okay not to have the answer, that we "don't know" and we are okay saying that.
> ⟩ Men asking for help, without making up a story that this means we "aren't manly."
> ⟩ Men seeking contributions from others in making decisions.
> ⟩ Men caring for others.
> ⟩ Knowing that being a man has nothing to do with our sexual orientation, and that we don't need to be sexually dominant to prove our manhood.
> ⟩ Recognizing that men with disabilities are men.
> ⟩ Believing that our job (or lack of one) doesn't define us as men.

It's up to you to decide which of these, if not all of them, can be considered in your own evolving sense of being a man. Regardless, these rewritten healthy masculinity attributes are available for you as you see fit. So, if you are ready, there are some simple steps you can take right now to start your journey.

< CHAPTER TWO >

TOO OFTEN EXCLUDED VOICES OF MASCULINITY

When I was interviewing Mike Kaufmann, CEO of Cardinal Health, for the final chapter of this book, I asked him his views on healthy masculinity. Not only did he share them, but he also encouraged me to distinguish the voices of white men from other men, such as men of color, gay men, and men of other identities. What follows below are voices of masculinity that are often excluded.

As long as I have been involved in healthy masculinity work, I've been interested in how others view healthy masculinity—especially men that don't look like me, or ones that identify differently than me. When co-leading in the ManKind Project, I mentored several gay men, each of whom was exploring his own sense of masculinity and leadership. I had also started a multicultural men's group (in which I was the only straight, white man), its primary purpose being to create a safe place for all of us to do our work.

I recognize that when it comes to healthy masculinity, my views on allyship and leadership are just mine. I'm also aware that

< 23 >

a white guy like me, with privilege and a platform to bring other voices forward, has a responsibility to do so.

In the spirit of inclusivity, this chapter brings in healthy masculinity perspectives for the men reading this book who don't identify as white and/or cisgender. It also gives a wider range of voices the opportunity to share some advice on allyship with white cisgender men like me.

Each of these men are true heart-centered leaders and I consider it an honor to be able to have these conversations with them. My invitation for you in reading these excerpts is to simply listen. Avoid judgment. Stay in your heart and seek to understand their perspectives, recognizing that they each are on their own journey of healthy masculinity, just like you.

Let's meet them!

MIKE KAUFMANN

I met Mike Kaufmann in 2015 when he was CFO at Cardinal Health. Rayona Sharpnack, the Founder and CEO of The Institute for Women's Leadership (IWL), brought me onto the facilitator team to observe and bring forward "healthy masculinity" when appropriate. Mike was involved as an active executive sponsor for WIN, the Women's Impact Network. He supported training for men, which subsequently evolved into Gender Partnership workshops for both men and women.

Mike has since become Cardinal Health's current CEO. He is cisgender, white, male, and heterosexual.

‹‹ ››

When we spoke in early 2021, I asked: "What does healthy masculinity mean to you?"

Mike, without hesitation, replied, "Healthy masculinity starts with me . . . it's okay to be who I am." He went on to say, "It's okay *not to be in charge* . . . I'm fine with being in charge when necessary." Mike is "not afraid to be emotional. I'm okay to be teary-eyed. Half the stuff I talk about is teary-eyed! I can be stoic when I need to. I like to be right and [I'm] willing to be wrong. I am willing to be coachable—[to] not have all the answers."

Now that we have heard from Mike, let's see what the others have to say.

TOM BOURDON

Tom Bourdon, former CDO (Chief Diversity Officer) of Staples, lives in Australia with his husband and children. He was a guest on the Better Man Conference's Getting Real weekly live conversation series and is part of the Better Man community.

《　》

We talked in the spring of 2021. When I asked what healthy masculinity means to Tom, he responded that the term masculinity in and of itself presents a struggle; it leads him to ask, "Does your gender dictate masculinity?" As a gay man, masculinity feels uncomfortable to begin with. The tough guy image comes to mind, as masculinity has historical connotations of aggression.

By reframing it as healthy masculinity, anyone can embrace it regardless of gender. It can mean caring, having strength with respect to willpower, being persistent, and looking out for others. You don't have to be better than others—you can *uplift others.*

Tom later shared that to him, a big part of healthy masculinity is owning who you are, being okay with who you are, and having pride in who you are: "The pride component, in and of itself, is really huge. It's not at all about being boastful or thinking that you're better than others. But it's about loving yourself, and not having shame in what makes you unique but rather celebrating it—and then also having the capacity to recognize/honor/celebrate other people's uniqueness, as well."

It was an honest, heartfelt answer and it fostered a deeper connection between the two of us.

Tom then shared what healthy masculinity in action could look like. Profoundly and simply, to Tom, "masculinity is doing everything you can to uplift others, to be of support [to] others. It's hero-less." He posed the question, "Why can't masculinity be soft, caring, and uplifting instead of [these] being . . . traits that have been historically feminine?" My immediate answer: "It can be!"

Much that Tom shared is in alignment with the heart-based leadership principles we have thus far and will later discuss, and his views on healthy masculinity fly head-on in the face of the man box.

When we moved on to the topic of attributes that support allyship and leadership, Tom told me that empathy and the simple power of listening are two of the biggest ones that come to mind. (Little did he know that he was echoing the second step of the Ally's Journey, listening with empathy and compassion. More to come on listening in later chapters.)

Tom also offered that it's important to understand that we don't have all the answers. Everyone has their own answers. Allies and leaders can support others by holding space for them to find their own answers. There is no right or wrong, nor is there a need to be in charge.

I then asked, "What attributes will support allyship and leadership?" Tom answered that "Allies need to be able to act. It's a balancing act with emotions that should have you asking, 'How am I moving things forward? . . . How do I do this—with inclusivity?'"

Tom generously answered my last question, "What could allyship look like between straight men and gay men?" with three simple steps.

1.   Check in with them and ask, "How are you doing, and what can I do to support you?"
2.   Listen, as people will tell you what they need.
3.   Do it! Give people what they need, not what you think they need!

COREY PONDER

Corey Ponder is a tech professional who is passionate about doing what's best for the user; he works on technology platforms that foster community and creativity, and center equity. Based in the Bay Area, as a speaker and creator Corey uses the powers of empathy and community-building to connect people to their capacity to be better allies and create more inclusive spaces.

Corey is also a facilitator who has delivered allyship programs with the Better Man team. He is a Black, heterosexual man.

《 》

Corey and I caught up after co-delivering a workshop for a client. Corey's superpower is his ability to empathize. When I asked him, "What does healthy masculinity mean to you?" he responded with three words: "Emotion, vulnerability, and acceptance."

For Corey, "It's about not being afraid of having emotions or conveying them—whatever the range." He pointed out that *vulnerability* goes hand in hand with sharing emotions.

I asked Corey if he could speak to whether masculinity is different for a Black man. He shared that when he was younger, he was ashamed of being super high on the Myers-Briggs spectrum (a popular personality test) as a "feeler." He didn't think this facet of his identity was valuable; in his experience, emotional Black men weren't universally accepted among Black men, so he initially decided that it wasn't worth it to feel his feelings.

He later reframed this: "My feelings are going to help me survive. Being able to tap into them and how I am perceived in my environments when I experience them will actually help me." This made Corey think, "How can I put value on this?"

Corey's reframe evolved to knowing, "I have an ability to sense anger, fear, sadness. It's important to understand how I am perceived as a Black man. And I can be the man I want to be despite the stereotypes put on me. I can process these feelings in a more productive manner."

I asked Corey how things might be different for him as a Black man when it comes to showing his emotionality. He shared that he has had experiences where his emotional display was demonized or used against him because of his color. His "aggression, as an example, is viewed different than for white men."

Corey continued, "If I step into the power trap of using strength to demonstrate masculinity—there are different consequences [for] me as a Black man. Even being in touch with my soft side, in my communities of people of color, I want to show up with love and care. If I am not careful, I can be consumed amidst other interactions."

What Corey said made me think of my ability as a white man to speak my truth, be in my power, show my emotions, and have different consequences—never as severe as for a black man.

Our conversation made me more aware of what it means when I ask all men to be authentic. I now realize that men of color must consider their own authenticity and whether it comes at a cost. My white privilege is something I can use to support men of color.

This awareness also helped me to realize that us white guys can and need to make space for others to be safe and vulnerable without judgment, to practice and learn.

Lastly, I asked Corey, "What do you need guys like me to understand?"

He offered to me (and all of us) his wish for us to understand the fatigue of adjusting one's behavior to make others more comfortable, a habit he formed from internalizing microaggressions (microadjustments due to microaggressions). Corey illustrated his point: "I walk across the street ahead of someone that is [a] white female because I have learned over the years that in many instances, the person will display a sense of discomfort simply because I am a Black male."

Corey continued: "Even though it's automatic and these are the decisions I make every day, to the white men, my ask is, 'What labor are you doing every day to think about the subjective decisions you make? Are you considering your impact to others? Are you doing that same amount of labor that I am to be aware of your bias and privileged so as to not negatively impact others?'"

I thanked Corey and shared with him my deep appreciation for helping me to empathize with his exhaustion from emotional labor. Even more profoundly, he challenged me to up my game regarding the work it takes to be an ally. This made me think: "He's doing the work, so why shouldn't I put in the same amount of effort?"

Corey offered four steps for white male allies to follow:

1. Empathize with the exhaustion and trauma and gaslighting that people of color go through every day.

2.   Know that they consciously make adjustments every day and that too is exhausting.
3.   Ask yourself, "What am I willing to do to adjust my behaviors to minimize their impact on others?"
4.   If you are white, use your privilege to advocate for men of color when we are not in the room. Modeling heart-based leadership is an opportunity to influence. People will believe it because of your position as a white leader.

When I asked Corey if he had any guidance for men of color who might be reading this book, he offered the following:

1.   See your connection to emotions and empathy as a strength.
2.   See how you can influence and impact others.
3.   The sooner you recognize this, the better it is for all of us.

CHUIN PHANG

Chuin Phang is an inclusion and diversity leader (formerly with Pinterest), a previous attendee of the Better Man Conference, and an advocate for engaging men as part of a company's inclusion strategy. Chuin is a gay, Asian man.

《 》

It was refreshing to have a conversation with Chuin, as he answered the questions I had for him by aligning his answers to the four steps of the Ally's Journey—without me even asking!

To start off, Chuin shared that part of what healthy masculinity means to him is to be self-aware, to be willing to take a step back and think before you act. This is step one of the Ally's Journey, *acknowledge your stuff.*

Chuin told me, "Instead of reacting to adrenaline and being aggressive, to me, healthy masculinity is about flexing our new muscle to not act out physically. Positioning myself with humility and empathy. Healthy masculinity is . . . being willing to be wrong, to hear another's perspective." This is step two of the Ally's Journey, listening with empathy and compassion.

Additionally, Chuin connected healthy masculinity to privilege, saying that us guys with privilege need to share the stage by centering others.

I wanted to explore how different cultures might influence healthy masculinity. Chuin shared that as an Asian man, he was raised to believe that masculinity aligned with traditional gender roles, with men being dominant and women submissive.

Gay men are often seen as less masculine. Within the gay community, Asian men are also stereotyped as more submissive. For Chuin, masculinity as a concept is elusive, or fluid; it has led him to present or act differently in different situations. He went on to share that he may act one way with white men or another way with Asian men.

Chuin often finds himself having to negotiate his identity out of respect for his family and the older generation. He shared, "I have to be careful so as to not offend the older generation. Out of cultural respect, I won't call out the older generation. By coming out, and questioning my masculinity, to them it's considered selfish and an un-community act. This is because you are asking them to adjust their way of thinking. I choose not to do that."

I asked Chuin, "What do you want men seeking to become allies to hear from an Asian man?"

His answers were as follows:

1. Understand that words have an impact.
2. Do your homework so as to minimize their triggering impact. Be thoughtful. Know when to apologize, and—this is step three of the Ally's Journey—take responsibility.
3. Learn to read body language and signals.
4. Be comfortable with your own discomfort and fragility. Figure out a way to witness others and not flinch so as to not trigger others.

SEAN COLEMAN

Sean Coleman is the Founder and Executive Director of Destination Tomorrow, and a consultant and owner of Sean Ebony Coleman Consulting. Sean is a Black, transgender man. He has contributed to the Better Man Conference and is part of our community.

《 》

Sean and I had the opportunity to connect in the spring of 2021. I was eager to ask what healthy masculinity meant to him. He chuckled at first, but went on to say that it's being able to define what it means to be a man, unapologetically bucking the system, and not allow others to tell you how you should perform your masculinity. To Sean, "it looks like me being able to define my manhood and . . . move forward with other men [who] still uphold those toxic traits. It also is being able to have conversations about masculinity with these very same men."

He continued to say that healthy masculinity is about being in touch and in tune with your feelings, exploring them, and not allowing others to tell you how to feel. It's about being vulnerable and learning the lessons, especially with women in your life.

Uniquely, Sean had experiences prior to his gender transition that he could rely on to support him.

He encourages all of us (and me) that once you are doing the work, take the time to be visible and allow others to walk the journey with you. It helps to remove the stigma.

Sean had a few pointers with respect to allyship between men for men. He shared that it needs to be designed by the person who needs it. Similar to what Tom Boudon said, it's about asking a man what he needs, and then showing up: "As a Black trans man, you can ask me what do I need? Then show up!"

Sean wants white, cisgender guys to know that it's important for Black men to have a voice, not just Black trans men. We need to have deep discussions to better understand what Black men are experiencing. They are still seen as predators.

This will require that "We, Black men, need you all [white guys] to do your work."

My interpretation of what I heard Sean say made me realize that we, as white men, need to talk amongst each other and humanize what's going on—how we are complicit as opposed to being part of an anti-racism, homophobic, transphobic, sexist solution. We need to be completely honest about what truly is happening and who it is happening to. It's about using platforms to speak out. If we have an audience, we need to use our positions to voice our solidarity and act accordingly.

IN SUMMARY

By no means do the men I interviewed include all voices; they represent a common cross-section of men's voices and perspectives that I value. There are many other voices that I did not include that I want to name: brown men, men with disabilities, men who have served in the military or time in prison. Indigenous men. Young men. Neurodivergent men. Women's perspectives on healthy masculinity.

These conversations confirm a long overdue, much needed rebuke of toxic masculinity that aligns with a heart-centered rewrite of healthy masculinity. Many of these interviewees' reframing of healthy masculinity legitimize the hardest life skills to adapt to—such as empathy, the sharing and experiencing of emotions, vulnerability, and mindfulness.

Also hugely powerful is how each of these men offered what healthy masculinity looks like in action: listening to, uplifting, and supporting others; allowing others to take charge and make decisions; and doing your own work around bias and privilege, to the degree that you become aware—by virtue of your own labor—of how you impact others.

Several of my colleagues and friends rendered guidance for white men seeking to become better allies and leaders. My invitation to you is to keep their words in mind and heart as you progress through the book.

CHAPTER THREE

SIMPLE STEPS
TO TAKE RIGHT NOW

ecoming an ally and inclusionary leader is a journey. If you
are like most men, you probably want to know, "Where do
I start? What do I do?" Good! These are totally normal questions
to ask. I'm not going to answer them right off, because part of
the process requires you to see and consider a story that illumi-
nates what *not* to do. I recommend that you slow down, hold
your enthusiasm to get started, and read the following section
for some context.

I chose this story to magnify the damage that silence can inflict.
While sexual harassment in the workplace does still occur, what this
story illustrates is how the behavior of one man can have a rippling
effect on an organization and its individuals. Most importantly, what
I want you also to consider is the silence of others and how their
complicity fails to protect their own.

This story is not the example of many; it does serve to illustrate
how silence in various forms can be damaging.

SILENCE IS NOT GOLDEN

Jimmy Carter once said, "Silence is as deadly as violence. People of power, privilege, and moral conscience must stand up and say 'no more' . . ." For anyone wondering if they should speak out or not, just remember: Dictators and abusers survive when good people do not speak out.

For many men, having power, privilege, and moral conscience is a given. Silence can no longer be the norm—in your workplaces, in your community, and in your families—when it comes to sexist and racist behavior by other men. Instead of being the silent majority tainted by the actions of a few, it's time for us men collectively and individually to stand up against inequity. If we don't, it's a reflection on us.

Silence can be individual or it can be a collective agreement. Regardless, silencing a transgression, a misuse of power, a micro-aggression, or sexual harassment—at any degree of harm—can fester and only adds to the initial hurt. Silence perpetuates harm. Most men aren't aware that over time, various forms of silence, lack of recognition, and little appreciation of difference slowly erodes safety, trust, and the willingness of women and marginalized folks to bring their full selves to work.

Once this occurs, a company's culture is likely compromised, making it more difficult for the nondominant groups (women and marginalized folks) to be as effective as they are capable of being. At this point, the company suffers along with those individuals.

THE SOUND OF SILENCE

There was a time when men's sexual harassment and misconduct were tolerated or covered up in the workplace, government, sports, and the entertainment industry. The tolerance and cover-up were all about "protecting the franchise," the revenue, the brand. Whatever it took to "make it go away" *was the norm.*

It was simply too risky for women to come forward, as there was no clear path to be vindicated or protected, or to advance one's career. What was certain to occur: shame, denial, loss of career opportunities, and continued emotional stress. So, what did most people do? They stayed silent.

While the current social and political narrative, fueled by Time's Up and Me Too and strong women's movements, has swung the pendulum in the other direction, there is still much work to be done by men when it comes to examining their behaviors and the respective impacts on women. And in an interesting and ironic twist, the perception of men, albeit obscured, is that men currently seeking redemption for past transgressions aren't finding a path forward other than career annihilation. This is their perception, so what do they do? They remain silent in the dark. The following story is not just about one man; it's about those around him and the role they played. When reading this, resist your temptation to say to yourself, "I'm not like Mark." Instead, ask yourself if you can identify with any of the other players when it comes to general sexist behavior. Maybe you can own some of your personal tendencies. I say this not to shame you, but to get you thinking.

Mark was the number one broadcaster in the newsroom, according to most polls. He was well liked, and his viewership fueled lots of advertising dollars. Behind the scenes, it was common knowledge that when Mark's door was closed, knocking was not an option. He was the star of the show and pretty much everyone bent over backwards to accommodate this powerful man's needs and quirks, including looking the other way.

Under the cover of his seductive smile, charm, and the revenue he was responsible for, Mark could get away with just about anything. Mark was married, but he couldn't resist his own internal tendencies to seduce or coerce other women who came into his view at work. When a young and eager woman joined the production crew, she would often end up in his studio room.

One day, just like numerous others, a determined and aspiring career woman named Amy fell under Mark's spell. Capitulating to the power differential, she found herself saying yes when she never intended to. Initially, *she tried to stay silent*. She didn't tell anybody until the pain was too great, at which time she went to HR and one of the studio execs. They listened and said nothing; one of them dismissed Amy's complaint of sexual harassment altogether. They offered her a new position. They offered her money to stay silent. And just to make sure she got the message: Unless Amy accepted their offer, they promised her career in the industry would be finished, effectively blacklisting her. *They remained silent.*

When the silence at the top leaked outside the company, all hell broke loose. The studio was forced to fire Mark.

It was only then that the collective silence was uncovered. Mark's female costar Adrian knew. When Adrian first started on the job, she engaged in a "relationship" with Mark that ended with Mark starting a relationship with another woman. Adrian could have reported him or warned the next woman. She did neither for fear of it negatively affecting her career. She would see this pattern repeat several times over a five-year timeframe. Adrian's silence, while painful, allowed her to progress in her career. This didn't stop the growing resentment and lack of respect she had for him. So, when his misbehavior was revealed and he came to her for support, Adrian finally said no.

Each time a new young woman gave notice, the producer, Jason, knew what to do. He had conducted many of these exit interviews already. Not much was said by the women, nor did he ask. He offered to write a good recommendation. Most women declined.

When it came to hiring new candidates, Mark asked in advance to see resumes and headshots, and based on candidates' pictures, advised Jason on which women he wanted to interview.

The rest of the men on the production team knew what was going on, as well. They toed the line because that is what they saw modeled and it was what the culture supported. They, too, stayed silent.

When silence of this magnitude occurs, it's not just women who are harmed. The silence affects the women who were harmed prior, the other women trapped in the organization's culture that tolerates this type of behavior, and finally, men who were unaware and thus not complicit—but who get categorized as part of the problem.

While stories this egregious are less common in corporate cultures today, they do still occur. Men's behavior, gone unchecked, can still cause harm, making it less safe for women and folks who belong to nondominant groups to bring their whole selves to work. Throughout this book, everyday occurrences of men's behaviors as leaders and allies will be examined so men can, with new awareness, adjust their behavior to make it more in line with being a respected leader and ally.

Seeking to Understand: What Happened?

This is a story about a man in a position of power and privilege, and how he misused it. It is also about his failure to understand the *power differential* he held over vulnerable women in lower positions. Beyond that, it's about *hidden sexual behavior* that impacted another human being. *Showing Up* seeks to shine positive light on how to consciously use (as opposed to misuse) this same power and privilege for good. It also seeks to equip men to get out of the rut of silence—which, along with complicity, is at the center of this story.

Mark probably thought he wasn't doing anything wrong by simply pursuing a woman he considered attractive. After all, he had done it countless times before and nobody said anything. For Mark, *others' silence* indicated that nothing was wrong with his behavior. Why wouldn't he keep up his sexual conquests?

It never occurred to Mark how the power afforded to him as a result of his position in the company, along with his corresponding privileges, might influence another person—especially a younger person in the organization, a woman, toward whom he made advances. He never placed himself in her shoes, because if he had, he just might have been able to fathom her biggest fear, the question she was sitting in: "What will happen to me and my career if I say 'no' to his advances?" This is what most men in Mark's position fail to consider. It ends up being their downfall. (I will further address this failure to see the power differential and its impact in the learning section to come.)

Male leaders are best served by avoiding personal relationships in the workplace when there is a power differential because, no matter what, their position and its resulting power will always weigh over the subordinate. No amount of good intent and charm can change this.

There was no company policy against personal relationships between employees, so technically Mark wasn't in violation. But that is not the point.

In June of 2018, Intel Corporation signed on as a sponsor for the Better Man Conference. I was quite excited to have them come on board. The excitement was short lived: The very day I was informed of our new partnership, CEO Brian Krzanich stepped down for violating the company's nonfraternization policy. An investigation had determined that he had engaged in a past consensual relationship with a woman.

What is important to note, especially for male leaders, is that consent is a slippery slope. Just because a woman has verbally consented misses the point because the power differential is always present and that, more often than not, limits a woman's opportunity to "say no" for fear of career-ending consequences. As long as there is a hierarchical difference in position, in which the man is higher up in the organization, that unspoken influence will always be present . . . for the woman.

Also important to note is Intel's commitment to creating equality in the workplace. That same day Krzanich stepped down, my contact at Intel assured me that their commitment to our partnership and the movement I was leading was still important to them, especially in light of the circumstances. They have been a partner ever since.

Sometimes, a woman with tremendous courage chooses to speak up. For our character Mark, this one woman who decided to buck the trend and courageously speak up was met with redirection and questioning. This woman had no allies. Nobody there to listen with empathy and compassion, to validate her experience, to protect her and shield her from fallout as a result of her reporting what happened. She was alone.

Unfortunately, leadership had one job to do, in their minds: protect their star and the company if the story got out. They offered her a promotion, more money, to keep quiet. They threatened to end her career. This is what they always did, because the silence is what worked. The big miss here is that the company failed to protect women from these occurrences.

Patriarchy protects its own as a matter of survival. This scenario happened because the organization—run largely by men—put men over women and money over culture, choosing to support an individual over the collective. It also happened because, until fairly recently, occurrences like this were suppressed, covered up, or flatly denied. It was acceptable—by the standards of men in power.

What happened to this woman? What consequences did she face? She was taken advantage of sexually, for starters; no one who has not experienced such a thing can ever really understand it. Second, she carries the shame that comes with it, the shame others project onto her, and ultimately she underwent a career-ending event, whereby she will only be remembered for reporting the sexual transgression that took Mark down. Hard to recover from.

The consequences to Mark? The company? Jason? The other women and men who still work at the company?

Mark now is blacklisted from the industry, his future essentially over . . . just like hers. Worse yet for him, Mark still has yet to grasp the undue influence of his power over her that made it difficult in her mind to say no. He maintains he did nothing wrong, that an example is being made of him. Clearly, empathy for her or any other woman is not within his reach.

As for the consequences to the company, several long-standing advertisers called to share that they would not renew their contracts. Some didn't even call. Some pulled their contracts on the spot. The company's revenues and reputation suffered. Adrian sought to get out of her contract and with that, the company settled with her for a tidy sum. The executives who offered Amy a new position and hush money were replaced.

While Jason felt bad for the women who left, he also didn't feel good about bringing in another new hire that he would eventually replace. Yet he remained silent. Eventually, even Jason couldn't continue perpetuating this pattern of Mark's. Jason gave notice and after several failed attempts to secure new employment, he left the industry. Word got around, and nobody was willing to hire him—just like Mark.

Yet the other women in the organization still don't feel safe because within their culture, there is still silence.

What about the other men who were complicit? Men are often influenced by their male leaders and the tone that they set. If male leaders model silence, men largely emulate it. This doesn't make it right; it simply lends credence to why it occurs.

But what about the silence of other women? Occasionally, senior women who have endured similar situations chose to remain silent in the interests of their own desired career advancement. They pay a big internal price. What many women in this position don't realize is that their silence keeps the door open for other women to have the same experience.

We learned that Adrian, Mark's costar, was one of his conquests. The difference here is that she kept quiet and managed to climb the corporate ladder. She played their game and ended up having too much to risk. Her silence slowly ate at her while it simultaneously perpetuated the victimization of others. Because Adrian chose to break her silence when Mark went to her for support, the company decided to go in a different direction and not renew her contract. It cost the company a lot of money to buy her out, as she knew too much. However, her career never really recovered. Worth noting is that she aged out, something that doesn't happen to men.

Adrian was in a no-win situation. Women I know who have had similar experiences have shared that shame—regardless of their innocence—plays a big role. The public blowback and anticipated consequences have kept many women silent. Slowly, that is changing.

I don't blame Adrian for her silence; what's most important is that we understand how damaging and far-reaching silence can be.

SO WHAT ABOUT THE REST OF US GUYS?
WHAT CAN WE DO NOW?

There will be many choice points along your path of becoming an ally and inclusionary leader. We've seen an egregious example of sexual harassment. There are many other behaviors by men that, left unexamined, make work environments less inclusive.

Using the example of Mark and the men who were complicit in their silence: When it comes to being the best ally and leader, how do you want to be seen and experienced, and what are you willing to do about it?

As an ally, it's more than sexual behavior or violating a non-fraternization policy—these are just a few examples of many. It's what you do or don't do when a guy makes a sexist or derogatory comment, either in the company of a woman or not. Whether you choose to use your position as a leader to invite a woman's voice into the conversation at a meeting when she is the only woman in attendance. If you ask a woman to set up the meeting space with coffee, or if you do it yourself. It's whether you see an issue with there being no women candidates in the pipeline of new employees to hire.

Silence in any of the aforementioned scenarios causes similar harm to women.

Many men inside companies aren't aware of how their language and behavior impact what women experience as a result, however small. That is because silence (or tolerance), up until now, also permitted these behaviors and language to continue. Most guys just keep being guys without giving much thought to the experiences of those around them, because those are not their lived experiences. Too often, men get a pass. Too often, they give a pass. The idea behind this arrangement is that if I give you a pass now, I get one later. This is all unspoken.

Most guys aren't aware of their male privilege and what it affords them. Nor have they given much thought to how societal norms of masculinity drive their choices. Have you?

Not too unlike Mark (or the other men in the organization), many men are unaware that they were saying or doing anything wrong. And to be clear, I'm not saying that most men *have* done anything wrong. But to do nothing when the people around you are impacted by the misbehavior of other men isn't okay either.

The story about Mark illustrated how the choice to keep instances of sexual harassment silent can hurt a lot of people, including the organization itself. The news about Intel showed how the very existence of a power differential—despite supposed consent—is not tolerated by a company, and how that company did what was necessary to keep folks in nondominant groups safe.

While these two areas are important parts of the puzzle, for now, let's look at the bigger picture of what it means to be an ally and inclusive leader in everyday life: both at work and at home, where the infractions are less obvious and ingrained in old behaviors that don't necessarily align with bad intentions. The following concepts and exercises will set you up for the Better Man Pledge and move you toward more drilled-down, specific organizational and individual progress that we'll discuss later on.

CLASS IS IN SESSION

I designed this section to help you think about several things that will focus and empower your journey toward becoming an ally and inclusive leader.

Many people (including men) avoid looking at the impact of their actions on their life, relationships, and career because sometimes the results are difficult to confront, emotionally and relationally. I'm going to assume that since you are reading this, you don't fall into that category. And it's okay if part of that statement reluctantly rings true.

Being a male leader, manager, or individual contributor in today's current social and political narrative means to have the spotlight on what you say and do. But *this attention from others on your behavior is rarely a motivator to change/adjust one's behavior.* I don't know about you, but this type of attention puts me on the defensive, and I'm less apt to change.

Maybe you feel powerless to change; maybe it seems easier to look the other way or blame someone else. One thing is for sure: If you take this approach, you are inviting a personal wake-up call. There is another option. It requires a leap of faith and a commitment to do the work, and I can share with you that it's well worth it.

Consider this a growth opportunity.

The more intention you put toward areas that need your attention, the more power you have to change them. This is more my style, and I hope it's yours too!

For the men reading this, I'm going to introduce you to some basic concepts that will support you in taking some simple steps toward becoming an ally and inclusionary leader. Each of these concepts has an intended positive effect—in your life, leadership, and in your organization.

There are some simple steps you can take right now. To start, it's about refocusing your attention. If you agree to do these things, they will set you up for the Better Man Pledge at the end of this chapter.

Put your behavior, language, and relationship with power under the microscope.

A big part of being an ally and inclusionary leader is about *proactively* shining light on your behavior, language, and power. How do they impact others? This isn't something you can do alone. Everyone (including you and I) has gaps in their ability to see themselves, and enlisting the help of others to "help you see" what you cannot is both invaluable and necessary.

You can start by doing the following:

1. **Declare for yourself an intention to learn more about what drives your language and behavior— without self-judgment.** This is all about mindset and it will serve you throughout your journey. The positive effect of this intention is that you will begin to understand why you do what you do, as well as what is holding you back. When you get curious about what drives your behavior and language, especially when they produce less-than-desirable results, you can rewrite your own narrative—and act and speak as an ally and inclusionary leader.

2. **Seek a female mentor/partner and get curious about her experiences and how she is impacted by men's behaviors.** There are numerous positive effects to doing this. Inviting a woman colleague or partner (or both) to give you feedback demonstrates a willingness to learn, to be better, and to be an ally—in her eyes. Second, your intention to be curious about *her* experiences as a woman will help you develop your empathy

muscles. This is not about putting the burden of your learning on women mentors; rather, it's about developing both personal and business trust that contributes to a beneficial relationship with them.

3. **Seek and secure a male support accountability partner.** Leadership positions are predominantly filled by men, and there are numerous times when women are not present—yet behaviors that are unbecoming of an ally and inclusive leader still may be. By partnering with a man as a support accountability partner, you can develop your ability to give and receive feedback in support of your growth as well as his. Having an accountability buddy ensures your continued growth. Your organization benefits as more men become woke.

4. **Learn about and understand the concept of power differentials and how others may experience your power and position.** Your leadership position at your company yields power over others, even when it's not your intention. It's important that you understand how this power can influence others, despite good intentions.

Power differentials (which are felt most keenly by the person with the least amount of organizational control) are made up of two ingredients: the actual control over others granted by your position/title, and an individual's own past experience with authority. *What is important to learn here* is that women and marginalized folks feel it, even when they're not aware they're feeling it. They live with it every day.

And here's why it matters that you know this: Whenever we're in a relationship with someone who has power over us, we do what we need to do to keep ourselves safe. To the extent you can, imagine the shoe being on the other foot. Your female superior—the woman you report to—makes a suggestive advance after hours while on a business trip. She possesses the ability to promote or demote you. Can you feel the lose-lose tension if you say no? If you say yes? I use this rarer example to support you in understanding what a lot of women go through.

When men in leadership fully understand this dynamic, they can use their power for good. Women and marginalized folks can then feel safer and more valued, which contributes to their ability to bring their whole selves to work; and organizations can benefit from more highly effective employees.

> Learn to connect to your emotions consciously instead of stuffing or not acknowledging them.
>
> You might be wondering why this is important. Unless we connect to and experience our emotions, they often unconsciously control our actions and language. Part of being an ally and inclusive leader requires that you feel, so that you can empathize with others. In chapter four, I will support you in cultivating emotional literacy with specific exercises; this is step one of the Ally's Journey, "Acknowledging Your Stuff." In the training section of this chapter, I will introduce you to an exercise to connect to your emotions.
>
> Men's life training on feeling and experiencing a range of emotions is virtually nonexistent. For most of you—if you are anything like me and the thousands of men I have worked with over the years—your father (or stepfather),

grandfather, uncle, or male coach were the models you looked up to. Anger was predominantly modeled, but the other main emotions—sadness, fear, shame, and joy— often were repressed. Society and the media normalized this as well. There weren't emotionally healthy, demonstratively vulnerable men who showed us the way. For so long, what it meant to be a man did not incorporate emotions—it rejected them.

Note to women: The feeling exercises are available to you as you see fit.

Five Core Feelings/Emotions That I Want You to Learn

Accompanying each definition is some contextual relevance as it pertains to being an ally. The way I remember them is to say, using my five fingers, "mad/sad/glad/fear/ shame." Say that five times, counting them out using your fingers. I've taught thousands of men these five core feelings. Yes, there are others, but these are the main ones we can build from. I wish to acknowledge the ManKind Project, which taught me these five core feelings so that I can teach them.

> **ANGER (MAD): You can't get what you want. Something is blocking it. Something is in the way.**

This is the one emotion that men know the most, and also the one that most often gets them in trouble. Anger is a complex emotion that I will explore more deeply in the next chapter. For the purposes of this section, I just want you to understand, at a base level, that anger is one of the core five emotions.

What I can share with you now is that most men aren't familiar with the relationship that anger has to underlying feelings of sadness, fear, or grief; and because most men don't know how to express these emotions, anger can become the go-to. As a result, when men exhibit anger, it often results in women feeling unsafe. I know this from personal experience: When I get angry, it scares my wife of twenty years, and she doesn't feel safe. I will share an exercise with you in the next chapter that will teach you how to release your anger. In the training section of this chapter, as a starting point, I will introduce you to a practice to simply connect to your anger.

> SADNESS/GRIEF (SAD): You had something/someone very important and now it's gone.

For women and marginalized folks, the painful experience of being excluded, minimized, and not seen for who they are is real. The only way you can empathize with them is through the ability to acknowledge your own sadness and grief. The pandemic has brought forth catastrophic loss for everyone and might be a place for you to connect to your own sense of loss. Maybe you can recall a time when you were excluded. (Exercises in the training section will help you better understand this.)

> JOY (GLAD): You have what you want, and you are happy.

There is immense joy awaiting you as you embark on your journey of being an ally and inclusive leader, especially when others acknowledge your kindness, empathy, and support.

> **FEAR:** Something is coming and it's dangerous. It's going to wipe you out.

This emotion triggers in most men (and women) a fight, flight, or freeze response. What is most typical, especially in light of the current social and political narrative, is "freeze"—which equates to silence. And as you have learned, silence can be interpreted as complicity and is not becoming of an ally and inclusive leader. The exceptions are those with PTSD and veterans. I will show you how to change your relationship to fear in chapter four.

> **SHAME:** There are two types of shame: healthy shame and toxic shame.

Healthy shame informs us when we're violating another person's boundaries and dignity, and can attune us to how we're affecting people. Toxic shame is that painful, sinking feeling telling us that we're flawed or defective. A positive opportunity/outcome of shame is that it tells us when we've hurt someone or crossed a boundary. This can and will occur, despite good intentions.

The journey of being an ally and inclusive leader is fraught with instances where we are going to make mistakes. Therefore, there will be the temptation and potential triggers to go down the rabbit hole of shame.

Shame may arise naturally when we've broken the interpersonal bridge, having spoken or acted in a way that has fractured trust or wounded a relationship. Consider shame as an alarm clock that awakens us and grabs our attention. If we can pause and notice it rather than plow forward, we have an opportunity to correct our behavior.

TRAINING SECTION

This section is about practice. It's also about preparation for the journey that lies ahead. I'm going to introduce you to your five core feelings with an exercise that will connect you at an emotional level to the Better Man Pledge, which I will subsequently walk you through.

Connecting to your emotions/feelings isn't something men were taught in school. Nor were we taught by the men in our life. That is because what was taught, emulated, tolerated, and even advanced was the complete opposite: not to feel our emotions; that they were bad. Worse yet, we were taught that to show them to others implied you were weak, soft, or gay (in a homophobic sense).

I am here to tell you that healthy embraces having an awareness and a conscious relationship to our emotions. The exercise below is designed to introduce you to your body below your chin—where your feelings exist!

INTRO TO FEELINGS EXERCISE
(ADAPTED FROM THE MANKIND PROJECT)

Have you ever heard, "You need to be more in touch with your feelings," or "You need to learn how to express your feelings better," or "I don't know where you're coming from half the time"?

It's not that men don't want to express feelings. We don't know how, haven't been shown how, or haven't been given permission. Feelings exist in our bodies. We feel our feelings in our bodies. Our bodies know what we feel before our minds do. Our minds learned to deny what the body knows.

Many have said, "The body never lies!" But early on in life, when a boy shows feelings, he hears: "What's wrong with you?" "Boys don't cry!" "Don't be afraid!" "Don't worry, be happy!" These messages teach us to ignore or distrust our bodies and our feelings. This way of thinking and relating to your emotions doesn't serve you in your personal life or as an aspiring ally and leader.

I've taught this exercise at retreats and routinely teach this to my coaching clients. A foundation of healthy masculinity is to understand your emotions—to connect to them and experience them—without judgment on your way to becoming more emotionally literate.

It's best if you find a location where you will not be interrupted and can raise your voice without alerting anyone. This exercise may feel silly; that's normal.

〉 Mad/Anger

1. Go back to a time in the past when you were really feeling mad/anger.
2. Close your eyes and see yourself in your memory. Recall what was going on.
3. Re-experience that feeling of anger in your body.
4. Locate in your body where you feel the anger.
5. Put your hand on the area in your body where you feel the anger.
6. Now, slowly take a breath into this feeling and experience it fully.

〉 Sadness/Grief

1. Go back to a time in the past when you were really feeling sad or grieving a loss.

2. Close your eyes and see yourself in your memory. Recall what was going on.
3. Re-experience that feeling of sadness/grief in your body.
4. Locate in your body where you feel the sadness.
5. Put your hand on the area in your body where you feel the sadness.
6. Now slowly take a breath into this feeling and experience it fully.

❯ Glad/Joy

1. Go back to a time in the past when you were really feeling happy or felt joy.
2. Close your eyes and see yourself in your memory. Recall what was going on.
3. Re-experience that feeling of joy/gladness.
4. Locate in your body where you feel the joy.
5. Put your hand on the area in your body where you feel the joy.
6. Now slowly take a breath into this feeling and experience it fully.

❯ Fear/Afraid

1. Go back to a time in the past when you were really feeling afraid or feeling fear.
2. Close your eyes and see yourself in your memory. Recall what was going on.
3. Re-experience that feeling of fear.
4. Locate in your body where you feel the fear.
5. Put your hand on the area in your body where you feel the fear.

6. Now slowly take a breath into this feeling and experience it fully.

〉 Shame

1. Go back to a time in the past when you were really feeling shame.
2. Close your eyes and see yourself in your memory. Recall what was going on.
3. Re-experience that feeling of shame.
4. Locate in your body where you feel the shame.
5. Put your hand on the area in your body where you feel the shame.
6. Now slowly take a breath into this feeling and experience it fully.

Why Did I Do Those Exercises? How Do They Help?

Consciously connecting to your emotions in an exercise like the one you just did probably felt foreign to you, maybe even silly. At the same time, this is necessary if you are going to be an aware and awake ally and inclusive leader. Outside of the workplace, the ability to connect to your emotions—to experience them instead of simply reacting to them—will also serve you in your personal relationships.

As said by British politician Andrew Bennett, "The longest journey you will ever take is the eighteen inches from your head to your heart." The journey to your emotions in your heart and body is an experience that, though perhaps new to you now, will always be available to you. While it is the road less traveled, it gets easier over time.

What you just accomplished, maybe for the first time, is bringing consciousness to actual emotions that reside in your body—*with intention.*

When I first did this exercise, it felt foreign to me, too. When you are able to locate and feel an emotion in your body, you make it possible to respond instead of react. Most men, due to a lack of teaching and modeling around emotional literacy, stuff their feelings or disconnect from them.

This virtually guarantees that at some point, a strong reaction will occur—usually at the expense of someone else. Maybe this has happened to you before?

This tool of emotional literacy is one of the principles of heart-based leadership. Being an ally and an inclusive leader will routinely invite feelings of fear, sadness, shame, anger, and even joy. Connecting to your own emotions takes away their power to run your actions and language unconsciously. This will allow you to relate to others, empathize with them, and ultimately be an effective leader and ally.

Everything you've done and read thus far has prepared you to fully understand and appreciate what you are saying and committing to when you take the Better Man Pledge. The pledge is a commitment that you are making to yourself, not to anyone else.

With your attention refocused, you are ready to step up to take another important step.

Taking the Better Man Pledge is akin to putting ourselves on notice that we are committing to being better. It's also a commitment to no longer remain silent. It is, in fact, a *personal choice to use our voice and make a commitment that we can live into as allies and inclusionary leaders.*

I invite you to recognize that this is a personal declaration to get interested in your communication and behaviors as they relate to women and marginalized folks. It also signals your new commitment to a certain way of being.

Maybe your company is volunteering your attendance for training. Maybe a woman in your life is calling you forward to do so. Maybe in thinking about your mother, wife, daughter, or son, you just decided it's time. All of these reasons are welcome.

Making the Taking of the Pledge Real

As a man among men, my invitation for you is to start your Ally's Journey right now by taking the Better Man Pledge.

1. First read to yourself and notice how you feel when you read it.
2. Write the pledge out on paper.
3. Read it out loud while alone.
4. Choose one woman you trust that you've identified as a mentor; ask for her support to witness you. Say the pledge aloud to her.
5. Choose a man (hopefully an accountability buddy) and read it out loud.

> **❯ Brief piece on "I" statements (Excerpted from the ManKind Project)**
>
> Sometimes the language of a culture teaches us not to take responsibility for what we are saying. Specifically, I make more sense when I use the pronoun "I" when I'm talking about what I want, what I feel, what I agree to, or what I believe. In society, we use another pronoun when referring to ourselves, the pronoun "you." Making an "I" statement denotes responsibility. Here is an example to illustrate.

HERE IS HOW IT SOUNDS WHEN I USE "YOU."

When you are the leader, you have to be careful about the words you use. Others are listening to you, and if you call yourself by the wrong pronoun, they get confused as to whether you are them or you.

By what pronoun did I identify myself, above?

So often, we tend to call ourselves "you," which makes clear communication difficult. "You" statements negate "I." "You" statements avoid accountability, integrity, and responsibility for feelings and actions. As a leader, I use "I" statements. I own my feelings and actions.

HERE IS HOW IT SOUNDS WHEN I USE "I."

When I am the leader, I have to be really careful about the words I use. Others are listening to me, and if I call myself by the wrong pronoun, they get confused as to whether I am talking about them or me.

Did you hear the difference that time? Which one was clearer? Which one was more powerful? I was speaking for myself.

With this new understanding of language and the power and responsibility of "I" statements, you are ready to take the pledge.

You've just been introduced to the five core feelings that support your own emotional literacy. Being an ally and inclusive leader is both a journey of mindfulness and heart, so that the head and heart can work together in partnership. If this feels like a leap of faith, it is!

I acknowledge that outdated man box behaviors have
no place in the workplace and that they need a rewrite with heart.
Concrete examples of these will be introduced in chapter four
along with the opportunity to learn new actions with heart.

I will challenge my old patterns
and no longer tolerate them in myself or others.
This will be covered in Step One of the Ally's Journey. You will
learn communication techniques that will support this.

In the spirit of my own emotional literacy, I will acknowledge fear,
feel it, and consciously use it to move me forward into the right
action, to be the man and leader I know I'm capable of being.
The Intro to Feelings Exercise, along with chapter four and exercises that address how to "work with fear" to resist silence and
more, all support this tenet of the pledge.

I will "do my work" with men so that I can continue
my learning and support other men, also using my power,
position, and privilege to engage other men in this movement.
This one aspect of the pledge will be supported by the important,
necessary step of not doing this work alone. Rather, do it with an
accountability buddy. Men engaging other men starts with you
modeling the behavior and inviting them to join you.

I will forever be an ally in training, recognizing that my bias
and privilege may occasionally cause harm to another person.
No matter how much you know and have learned, the only way
one can be considered an ally is when somebody else says so. I
refer to myself as "forever an ally in training" to keep me learning,
not to fall in the trap of thinking I'm "done." There are always
things to learn, and I know I'm going to make more mistakes

along the way. Chapter six will illustrate the impacts of your language and behavior and teach you how to clean up your missteps.

I will call out speech or behavior that negatively impacts marginalized people without shaming or blaming the person who acted or spoke.
Step Four of the Ally's Journey, "Think, Talk, and Act Like an Ally," will give you the guidance and tools you need to consciously combat man box tendencies by identifying them and then by acting from a place of healthy masculinity. You will learn in chapter seven how to think, talk, and act like an ally.

For Women and People Who Belong to Underrepresented Groups

I invite you to encourage men to adhere to the behaviors outlined in the pledge above. I also hope that you will allow for some likely missteps from men, while also simultaneously holding us accountable for fulfilling the journey.

A QUICK REVIEW OF WHAT YOU'VE ACCOMPLISHED

The work you've done in this chapter is foundational for your journey as an ally and inclusive leader.

You've had the opportunity to learn how silence, in the face of unhealthy masculine behaviors, can harmfully impact not only women but those complicit in corroborative silence.

You learned how the power differential by men in leadership can be misused. You learned how one company's president stepped down to maintain its zero-tolerance policy and protect its individuals, and how one company sought to protect the man responsible for causing harm.

You did the important emotional literacy work of connecting to the five core emotions I introduced you to.

And finally, upon learning about the power of "I" statements and the relevance of your emotions as an ally, you took the Better Man Pledge and made your commitment to being an ally and inclusive leader real by speaking it into existence and being witnessed by others in doing so.

Great job! Now, let's take a quick look at the key lessons you can take with you into the rest of the book.

> **Key Lessons**

1. You have a choice to put the spotlight of attention on your own behavior and language instead of waiting for someone else to do so.

2. Doing the work of being an ally and inclusive leader is not something you can do alone. You can partner with a woman mentor and seek an accountability male buddy to support your ongoing work.

3. When others are silent in the face of a perpetrator's unhealthy masculine behavior, it sends a message that the behavior is okay.

4. Silence in the face of unhealthy masculine behavior causes harm not only to those victimized, but to those who were complicit in their own silence. Organizations and their cultures pay the price by losing key people and clients.

5. Power difference is real, and women and marginalized people live with it daily. Most men

> don't have a comprehensive understanding of
> what it is and how it can be misused.
>
> 6. There are five core emotions to connect to: mad,
>   sad, glad, fear, shame. By connecting to them, you
>   can shift from reacting to responding and further
>   develop your ability to empathize.
> 7. You took the crucial step of making your
>   commitment real by taking the Better Man Pledge
>   and speaking it into existence.

Now, let's jump right into the first step of the Ally's Journey. We going to dive deep into several topics that are rarely front-of-mind for men—such as emotions, outdated man box behaviors, the influences of one's father, and privilege. It's time that men own these aspects of ourselves to make better decisions, improve our behaviors, and contribute to a better culture for all.

< CHAPTER FOUR >

STEP ONE
OF THE ALLY'S JOURNEY

Acknowledge Your Stuff

(NO SHAME REQUIRED)

P art of leading from the heart and supporting others in doing the same requires acknowledging our own stuff that gets in the way of desired behavior. This is the first step of the Ally's Journey. The "stuff" I'm referring to includes the unconscious influences that drive our behavior, our advantages (that is, privilege), as well as our emotions. For men, it also includes outdated man box behaviors, which don't serve men or the people around them. We'll go over each of these in this chapter.

Anyone and everyone can be an ally. Men can be allies to women, white people can be allies to people of color, heteronormative people can be allies to nonheteronormative people, and so on. With that said, we all need to acknowledge our differences in order to better understand the challenges others face in just being themselves. When we own our stuff, we make it safe for others to bring their full selves to work.

< 65 >

I'm also going to help you in this chapter by cultivating emotional literacy—a process that enables you to make new choices, use your privilege for good, and engage with others in a way that is beneficial to everyone around you. In the prior chapter, you were introduced to the five core feelings/emotions that will support you in this chapter.

Why Owning Your Stuff Is Important

The first step of the Ally's Journey is about getting interested in what drives our behavior. Much of this may not be obvious to you, which makes it even more important to look at. Becoming aware of these drivers allows you to consciously change your behaviors to be a more effective ally and inclusionary leader. Awareness and acknowledgement give you a glimpse into what might not be on your radar, and therefore ignored. The journey of becoming an ally requires you to look inward and be curious about what's motivating your language, choices, and actions. It is this exploration that will help you adjust your behavior to better support your leadership, both personally and professionally.

Men, operating from an outdated playbook of what it means to be a man, often struggle to grasp how their behaviors affect women in the workplace. And if the consequences of men's actions aren't brought to their attention, they don't directly connect to the experiences of women or underrepresented people.

For men, this unconsciously sets up a scenario where they just keep doing what they have always done. Unfortunately, the people around them are the ones most negatively and painfully impacted. Part of the solution is to present the experiences of women without shame or blame, giving men a chance to practice empathy in order to make changes in their behaviors. In fact, the solution is the same for all people who may not be showing up as allies simply because they aren't aware. I mentioned "presencing the real-life experiences of others" in chapter one.

I don't blame anyone for being unaware. It isn't my intention to give anyone a free pass, but shame isn't constructive, either. Instead, I invite you to consider that there is much that you might not know. That's okay. But you do have to get curious about "how you tick" and choose to take action about what's not working in order to grow.

What's in It for Me?

The benefits of "acknowledging your stuff" in your personal and professional life are numerous. Becoming aware of why you do what you do is powerful because you can then change your language, thinking, and actions for the better. Doing this work will likely improve your relationships, grow your leadership ability, and encourage more people to trust and follow you. By addressing the unconscious patterns driving behaviors that create challenges in your life, you will also probably feel better, experience more success, and expend less energy dealing with negative repercussions of your behaviors. You may even enjoy a sense of personal fulfillment. And in a business sense, you will gain more effective contributions from the people you lead.

THE BETTER MAN: A STORY TO CONSIDER

As a coach, leader, and facilitator, I come across many situations wherein men in various leadership capacities received feedback about their behavior and language due to their unexamined bias, privilege, emotional outbursts, and man box behaviors.

Most of these men were completely unaware of how they were being experienced, and upon hearing it, found themselves in a wake-up call opportunity. Fortunately, these men I coached made the wise choice to answer their wake-up call and self-examine, getting to the root of what was driving their behavior. What follows is an example of what it means to be a better man, in support of becoming an ally and inclusive leader.

I share this story because the person at its center represents many men—perhaps the *better man*, the type of man who, upon receiving feedback about his behavior, would choose to answer his wake-up call. Some of you will hopefully use this story to be a bit more honest with yourself and not wait for a wake-up call moment. I'll own that I am assuming positive intent about you, the reader, if you are a man.

The managing partner of a local law firm that had sponsored the Better Man Conference called me one day and asked if I would coach one of his partners. This particular partner, while valuable to the firm, had prompted enough feedback by women (and some men) about his lack of awareness of how he was being experienced by others to prompt the firm to require he address the feedback by getting some coaching. This coaching client was on the cusp of becoming an equity partner to his firm. His current behavior, unless it changed, would prevent him from moving forward.

This client, whom I shall refer to as Jim, epitomized being unaware of how he was being experienced across many fronts. A hard lesson—not being made equity partner—was beckoning; he could defend and deny or suit up and do the work necessary to change the narrative at his firm. This also meant he needed to change his own internal narrative.

Jim is a successful partner who brings in good revenue and wins many cases for the firm. However, during times of stress,

Jim got angry and lost his temper. His behavior in these instances, primarily with the women on the support staff, came across as condescending, impatient, and borderline authoritarian. When I interviewed the managing partner and one of Jim's female mentors, they shared that many women on staff felt unsafe, not seen or valued, and talked down to. Several said they no longer wanted to work with him under these conditions. There were even a few male partners, one man of color and one openly gay, who experienced similar instances of Jim's behavior. Upon hearing from some of the women they worked with who complained about Jim, they would not support Jim to become equity partner.

The information from each of these people was enough for me to arrange to meet with Jim, a white, male, heterosexual man. Rather than invite Jim to tell his story or version of what was reported, I asked him: Upon hearing this, what was his reaction and what did he want to do as a result? Jim shared that he was afraid his ability to become an equity partner was in jeopardy, that he was surprised by the feedback, and most importantly, he was willing to do whatever it took to improve his reputation at the firm. As was the case with Jim, more often than not it's others who highlight your behavior because they are impacted. Jim took advantage of this wake-up call opportunity and sought coaching. As I mentioned in the prior chapter, one step you can take right away is choosing to put your behavior, language, and relationship with power under the microscope.

I let Jim know that my coaching approach would be quite different. I shared with him that the idea of healthy masculinity as a core driver would be part of his coaching experience. We would examine his biases and man box influences, explore his privilege to better understand it, and go through some emotions and their relevance to his leadership. I also shared with him a coaching principle: What you do here (in the work environment), you also do in your personal life (in your relationships). Learning that this principle goes both ways put Jim on notice: "All" of his behavior needed to be examined.

I asked him about what he witnessed growing up, how his father interacted with his mother. His dad made most, if not all, of the decisions. I asked Jim about his relationship with his father and in that moment, he paused, looked me in the eye, and shared that he never felt seen by his dad. His dad was dismissive of him and not around much. He had a lot of sadness but more than anything, he was angry.

I asked him whether his fiancée had ever given him feedback similar to what he heard reflected to him by women in the workplace. He looked me again in the eye, just like before, and said with a choked-up voice that he had. Some moisture appeared in his eyes. It was apparent to me that, at this moment, he was realizing something about himself. He shared that he had displayed anger at her, that he often acted like his father did with his mother, and that she told him that she didn't feel like a partner. She didn't feel included in important decisions. He was scared that his intended marriage to her was in jeopardy. This was another wake-up call in the making.

We continued to go deeper. I asked him if he understood his *privileges* as a white man. Jim looked at me kind of funny and shared, somewhat defensively, that he didn't understand the relevance of my question. (This is a typical question from lawyers, one that I have no problem being asked, because I went to law school.)

I shared with him that it didn't mean anything was wrong with him or that he had done something wrong. I walked him through the difference between earned and unearned privilege, and how once those with privilege become aware that they have advantages others don't, they can make conscious choices on how to use those advantages to support others, especially while in leadership roles. This made sense to Jim.

We talked about how his privileges of being white, male, and economically advantaged could be used to lift others up instead of maintaining separateness. Jim also made an effort to get to know his other partners with identities other than whiteness or heterosexuality.

Jim worked hard with me to examine and understand his biases, and how his behaviors were often driven by unprocessed emotions. I introduced Jim to the five core feelings. Together, we ran through the list of man box behaviors; he realized that several of them were operating in his life without his awareness. One that was particularly apparent for Jim was, "Real men don't show their emotions, but anger is okay." Jim recalled seeing this modeled by his father many times. Another that resonated was, "Real men make all the decisions." Again, behavior his father modeled. Jim told me this pissed him off. His father's anger wasn't okay with him.

I probed a little deeper around the anger, making it personal. I asked him, "What's true about your anger? Are you sad, afraid, grieving a loss?" He replied: "Ray, you're killing me!" Jim was joking, of course, but the wetness in eyes was again apparent. He shared that he was sad he wasn't close to his dad, and he also would become afraid when his dad yelled at his mom.

I shared with him in that moment something I learned a long time ago: "We are like our fathers, warts and all. Not until we can own how we are like him, especially those attributes we promised ourselves we would never take on, can we truly mature as a healthy masculine man."

Jim immediately shared his realization that he was just like his father in how he made all the decisions at home, mostly not including his fiancée. Instead of feeling and acknowledging the fear that was underneath his anxiety at work, he showed anger.

We looked at how Jim's command-and-control style of leadership, especially with the predominantly female support staff, distanced those around him and made them feel less valued. He started to realize that this was probably how his fiancée felt, too.

Slowly but surely, Jim began to change the experience others were having of him. His humility continued to rise, and I am happy to say that there is a "happy ending" to this story—Jim made equity partner and got married!

Seeking to Understand: What Happened?

This is a story about a good man who, because of his lack of awareness about his behaviors and how they were impacting others, found himself in a wake-up call that required a choice. His choice, in simplest terms, was whether to defend and deny or to accept the feedback and use this wake-up call opportunity to learn about himself and improve how he shows up in all areas of his life. For a man who loved his work and his family, and had a relatively high level of success, a lot was at stake; Jim made the right decision.

Unlike the previous story, in which in the CEO stepped down due to sexual misconduct, this example of a man being awakened to his unexamined bias, privilege, and man box influences is more common. Let's take a closer look.

Until Jim was put on notice by the managing partner, he had no idea of the impact of his behaviors. The realization that his opportunity to become an equity partner was hanging in the balance got his attention. Upon deeper examination, he realized that his impending marriage was also at risk. These two life scenarios led Jim to decide: *I'll take the road less traveled and put my behavior, language, and power under the microscope so I can make the changes that will result in my becoming the man I know I am capable of being.* (This is one of the things you can do right now.)

With several trials running concurrently, the stress level at the firm was quite high; it would trigger Jim, and given his lack of emotional literacy training, *his inability to self-regulate resulted in angry outbursts.* When his anxiety showed up, he would blame others, avoid taking accountability, and worse yet, step into the command-and-control type of leadership he had seen modeled by his father growing up. Jim often stood over various secretaries' desks, firing rapid questions, using language like, "I'm a partner in this firm, and you need to stop what you are doing to take care of this item." He made it clear to whomever he was addressing that she and others were there to work for him. *Jim's behavior toward women was reminiscent of what he saw with respect to how his dad interacted with his mother.*

Unbeknownst to Jim, what was really going on for him—on the inside—was that he was afraid: fearful that he would make a series of mistakes, be taken off the cases, and ultimately lose his job. None of these fears were considered at a conscious level until we talked it through. *Jim's temporary emotional immaturity drove his behaviors, and anger came out instead.*

The consequences to the support staff were numerous. They felt disrespected, blamed, afraid, not seen, and unappreciated. Some got angry and, eventually, they made his work their last priority. They talked to each other, and some of them shared their experiences with other male partners. For a while, nobody said anything to Jim; once again, there was silence at work that, for a little bit of time, perpetuated his behavior.

But his fellow partners were now aware of how he was treating the support staff. Initially, this new reality Jim invited upon himself actually created more stress. His sleep and work quality suffered. He brought this stress home, and it put pressure on his relationship with his fiancée.

Jim began to realize and own how his unconscious adaptation of certain man box "rules" were playing out in his life, both personally and professionally. He had seen these rules played out and modeled for him by his dad. Specifically, Jim was adhering to the rule, "Show no emotion, but anger is okay." Second, his command-and-control style of leadership and how he made decisions at home were in alignment with the rule, "Men make all the decisions."

Jim felt isolated, not supported, and his anxiety only worsened. To Jim's credit, rather than going at it alone and aligning with the man box rule, "Don't ask for help," Jim made it clear he needed mine.

He also felt some shame. I cautioned Jim to not go into a "shame spiral" and think of himself as a bad person. Rather, I invited him to remember that he is a good person who made some mistakes, and that just makes him human. I reminded him that his actions going forward would speak the loudest.

Healthy Masculinity: Men's Curriculum

Acknowledging your stuff requires that you explore and validate the existence of various types of unconscious influences that may drive your behavior, emotions, and language. This requires a desire to learn what these influences can be, as well as a self-examination—do these influences apply to me?—and a resolve to stay awake to keep them in check.

UNPACKING YOUR MAN BOX

I introduced you to the man box in chapter one, citing the work of Paul Kivel and Tony Porter. Young boys on the threshold of becoming men are most impressionable; when we ask them what the *rules of being a real man* are, we hear: "Always be tough, successful, confident, always have the last word, always be the leader." Probably the most prevalent rule they share is that "real men don't show their emotions."

These boys learned this somewhere. They saw it modeled. I saw it modeled. You likely have, too. Maybe you still adhere to some of them; maybe you reject them; maybe you have evolved some new rules that work better for you.

These young boys grow up to be men, becoming leaders, managers, directors, individual contributors, politicians. Unfortunately, some of their early childhood influences come through in how they interact with others. Being an ally and inclusive leader requires we examine which are working and which are not, in order to be the allies and leaders we are capable of being.

We often emulate what we saw from influential figures. In my work with male leaders, I see many of these behaviors show up in some shape or form.

Let's take a deeper, in-action look at your first exposure to these rules as you were growing up.

FATHERLY INFLUENCES

My first book, *Wake Up, Man Up, Step Up,* introduces the Five Fatherly Influences to support men in gaining awareness as to how what they witnessed of their father's or father figures' behavior, and how they were affected by it, may be present in their lives. This includes the absence of a father. A few of these five influences are relevant to your journey as an ally and inclusionary leader and are part of you "acknowledging your stuff." We are going to unpack three of them in support of your journey.

"How Your Dad Demonstrated What It Meant to Be a Man."

The first fatherly influence is how your dad demonstrated what it meant to be a man. When I was young, I listened to my father. I watched the things he did and how he treated others, including my mom and siblings. I watched him provide for us, and I witnessed his work ethic.

Maybe there wasn't a central male figure in your life on an everyday basis; it could have been an uncle, a coach, or a teacher who was your model. *Watching these men shaped your view of what it means to be a man.*

Here are a few questions to answer and reflect on:

> How did your dad (or equivalent male figures) model what a real man is?
> What healthy masculine traits did he show you?
> What unhealthy masculine traits did he show you?
> What masculine traits, both healthy and unhealthy, can you own as yours?

"How Your Dad Related to Your Mom."

A second fatherly influence that bears relevance to your journey as an ally and inclusive leader is how your father related to your mom.

What you saw your father or father figure do likely influenced how you relate to women. As with most men, your first exposure to witnessing a man and a woman relating to each other probably occurred in your home.

It may have been your mom and dad, your stepmom or stepdad, your grandparents, or your dad and his girlfriend. How your father respected the woman in his life—how he spoke to her, listened to her, and touched her—played a role in shaping how you are with women. Even television and movies brought men's previously acceptable behaviors that are no longer the norm to life on the screen.

When it came to disagreements, the way your father interacted relative with your mother is also important to note. Whether your father demonstrated love with words, physical affection, acts of service, gifts, or spending time together, or did not demonstrate love at all, how you relate to women bears his influence.

You may have developed a dark side as a result of what you saw. You may have seen some behaviors from your father or father figure that you abhorred and resolved never to repeat. Remember the suggestion to embrace the notion, "You are like your dad, warts and all!" This is one of those times.

Most young boys who witness their father verbally, physically, or emotionally abuse their mother are often limited as to what they can do to protect her. Did you experience pain due to your helplessness? The feeling may be worse if your dad shot you down when you attempted and failed to rescue your mom. (This was my own lived experience.)

If this describes your experience, the boy within you represses this helpless feeling. But it may come out later in life, typically in a similar form of abuse toward the women in your life or your significant other. Or you may act helpless around women.

You might have felt scared, angry, or sad after witnessing your father treat your mom in a negative way. It might have hurt you emotionally, and in an instant, you decided not to be like him. This may have happened unconsciously as you buried both the event and your decisions without fully experiencing your emotions at the time (e.g., helplessness, sadness/grief, fear, or anger).

Fast forward to the present and imagine a scenario with a woman in your life. She may be your wife. Your daughter. Your colleague. She might even be your boss. You may be repeating history by acting like your father—or not like him. For example, do you make decisions of importance in isolation, not seeking input from the women in your life or at work? Or do you avoid making any decisions because you are reluctant to self-advocate? It's important to recognize that, either way, you are *reacting*.

Many men with whom I work often witnessed their fathers belittling their mothers. As a child, they vowed never to do this; however, as adults, they belittle their wives—even if they don't want to. They say it's a reflex. Recognizing that they are imitating what they were taught helps break the cycle to make a new choice. If you don't know, you won't change your behavior.

This is an opportunity to become aware of these handed-down behaviors and grasp how they don't serve you in your interactions with women as an ally and inclusive leader. By noticing that you are acting like your father (or creating the exact opposite behavior), you may make a conscious choice to respond "proactively" from your adult heart versus your childhood-developed response.

When you choose your own way of responding, possible outcomes you may experience are improved intimacy and communication with your wife or girlfriend; healthy modeling for your sons and daughters; or being mentored by a female superior who actively supports you at work because she is no longer the target of your defiant behavior.

I encourage you to take some time to answer the following questions to help you examine your father's influence on how you relate to women, both consciously and unconsciously.

For now, I want you to approach these questions only with curiosity to uncover some answers. Then I'll offer you tools to actually deal with this old stuff that has been holding you back.

> How did your dad treat your mom (or stepmom or girlfriend)? Did he treat her with respect?
> Did your father honor your mother? If so, how?
> How did your father (or male equivalent) conduct himself in disagreements with your mother?
> Is there any connection to how you relate to your wife and/or daughter that is similar or opposite to how your dad related to your mother and/or sister?
> Notice and acknowledge the feelings that accompany what you recall. If you did something differently, what would be a more loving approach?
> Lastly, reflecting on your answers to these questions, have you/do you repeat this behavior with women in the workplace, to whatever slight degree?

"How Your Dad Dealt with His Feelings."

This is a big one. Being an ally and inclusive leader requires *emotional literacy*, one of the heart-based leadership principles I mentioned earlier in the book.

How your father (or father equivalents) did or didn't experience his emotions modeled how to experience or not experience yours. If your dad did not deal with feelings in the moment and stuffed them down—like most men do—chances are that in your adult life, you experience the outburst or "sideways" version of feelings, where they come out not in the way that is most ideal. Maybe you "keep them in check" or stay disconnected from them. Regardless, you were likely influenced by what you saw.

TO START: IDENTIFY EMOTIONS
YOU'VE BEEN STUFFING

As allies and inclusionary leaders, cultivating emotional literacy by dealing with your emotions healthily goes a long way to improve your life and relationships.

For this reason, I strongly encourage you to explore and commit to your own emotional literacy as you step into being the leader and ally you are meant to be. All leaders are people, and all people feel—sometimes, a lot. Becoming familiar with your emotions and understanding how you experience them are non-negotiable steps as you move forward. After all, emotional intelligence has become a popular subject that is gaining relevance in the business world. And it's for good reason.

Most often, people tend to stuff or repress feelings of *grief/loss, anger, fear,* and *shame.* The problem with stuffing your feelings is that they eventually find their way out.

Anger is a complex emotion that is often connected to other underlying feelings. It can be violently expressed through actions and words toward another. Often, when anger is outwardly expressed, it is a result of stuffed feelings like sadness, fear, or grief/loss—or all three.

Shame is also a complex emotion tied to underlying feelings such as sadness, fear, and grief/loss. When unacknowledged, this emotion can result in self-abuse and renders healthy relationships with oneself and others more difficult.

We learned with Jim that underneath his anger was *sadness* and *fear,* that oftentimes when he was actually feeling sad or afraid, or experiencing anxiety, anger was the emotion he predominantly expressed.

Now, let's do something with all these emotions so you can begin to move forward. It's one thing to consider our feelings; it's another to experience them from a place of choice so that you have power over them instead of them having power over you.

Emotional Literacy Tools:
Releasing Fear, Shame, and Anger

In the prior chapter, I introduced to you the five core emotions: mad, sad, glad, fear, and shame. I invited you to connect to them. These tools are the next step. As we saw with Jim, ignored or unfelt emotions can burst out and cause more harm than good. You have also contemplated where some of your emotional expression or lack thereof originates from.

As allies and leaders, you now understand that you're likely going to be triggered, get angry, make mistakes, feel shame, and even get scared. The opportunity here is to shift from reacting to responding.

You should also understand where some of these feelings come from in the context of your childhood. It's important to realize now that those around you—who you lead, who you report to, the members of teams to which you belong—are also going to have these same emotional experiences.

With a little work, you can shift how you behave to lead inclusively with your emotions. When you do this, you'll have achieved emotional literacy.

To help you shift from reacting to responding, I offer the following processes, which I learned at a Mondo Zen silent meditation retreat. Being an ally is going to frustrate, challenge, and cause you to second-guess yourself. It's also going to bring forward feelings of anger and shame that, if left unchecked, can dictate your behavior. Maybe someone brings something you said that landed on him or her negatively to your attention. Maybe a woman shared with you that she didn't feel included at a meeting. Maybe you are feeling some shame for not stopping another person from saying or doing something to the detriment of another. These are all opportunities to go inside and connect to what is really true for you.

By getting curious about your anger or shame when you feel it arise, you can take the "charge" off of it and make different choices about how you respond.

Exercise: Anger and Shame Release

Anger is often the only emotion that men have had the experience of truly feeling and the permission to express, albeit toxically. Inclusive leaders and allies are well served by getting curious about the underlying feelings that are fueling the surface emotions.

Stepping onto and staying on the Ally's Journey will, in no uncertain terms, put you in touch with your emotions. You will likely make mistakes that result in your language or actions impacting another person in the form of a microaggression. While that may not have been your intent, it has an effect. And when a person shares their experience of how they feel, it will likely trigger you.

When we get triggered, the first feelings that manifest are often anger or shame. This happens because we really do care about the person we hurt, but that emotional truth is often temporarily inaccessible. This is where our initial impulses to defend, deny, avoid, or shut down can occur—none of which serve.

The next time you are angry or feel shame, consider that these feelings are equivalent to the ringing of a bell that prompts you to go through these exercises.

In fact, I'm sure you can identify an incident or feeling (something that recently upset you) close to the surface, so you can practice this process here with me, now:

1. First ask, "What is true about my anger/shame? Am I
    afraid, sad, or grieving a loss?" Let whatever thoughts or
    feelings arise and just live as they are.

2. Notice the answer(s) and acknowledge them by seeing
    if you can connect to the emotion directly. Can you
    locate it in your body? Where is it? Take a breath
    into wherever it is in your body and allow yourself
    to feel it. To feel it is equivalent to experiencing and
    acknowledging the emotion fully.

3. Ask: "Who or what do I really care about?" When we
    connect to our own hearts, we answer this question in
    the affirmative, and it releases shame or anger because
    we have connected to a core emotional truth. To
    respond from a caring and loving place, we need to have
    made the effort to understand what's true for us. This
    truth can completely change how you act and respond
    to any given situation.

4. For example, what you care about could be your
    partner, spouse, child, your work, home—or it could
    also be yourself. Defining what you care about helps
    you shift from reacting to responding by getting to the
    core of what's really true.

5. Notice your answer(s) and acknowledge them. What
    you are looking to identify is how you truly feel
    about this environment or person (or yourself, if that's
    what you came up with in the previous question).
    Oftentimes, *it's that connection we have with another that
    gets threatened*—and as a result, shame or anger comes
    up. The idea here is to acknowledge what you care
    about in order to slow things down and get interested in
    what's going on inside you.

6.　Respond. Is there someone you need to communicate with and share who or what you care about? It could be a mentee, mentor, or someone that you witnessed act out a microaggression.

7.　Might you have imposed an act of microaggression on someone? Do you have something to clean up? (In Step Three of the Ally's Journey, I will give you tools to have a clean-up conversation.)

Without action, your intention is not adequate. This is your chance to make good on being a better ally, by showing up without the anger and shame that was driving your behavior before.

I often advise my clients that "this is the place" from which we shall strive to operate. Understanding what's true from a heart-centered, caring place can and will inform your language and actions—if you allow it.

Exercise: Fear Release

There is a strong relationship between fear and control. Rather than feel the fear, most humans will use control as a way to avoid fear and make themselves feel safe. Leadership based in control doesn't leave much room for collaboration and contribution. This is the opposite of what we're aiming for in our work here.

Our goal with this exercise is to avoid unconsciously reacting from fear. Think of this practice as a pattern interrupter, whereby instead of reacting to the fear like you always did previously, you confront the fear, feel it, and act courageously.

Being an ally to others can induce fear in those seeking to be an ally, especially men. Fear of saying or doing the wrong thing results in many men staying on the sidelines in silence, which sends a message of complicity. When you feel fear about messing up as an ally, this is the time to use this exercise.

1. Locate the feeling of fear in your body. For example, you might notice tightness in your stomach, a tingling in your arms or shoulders, or even tingling or twitching in your throat or face. Take a breath into it. This gives you the opportunity to experience the fear by feeling it, which is far different than avoiding the feeling of it. When we resist feeling fear, we invite counterproductive behavior.

2. Notice if you have thoughts about the fear. Ask yourself: "What is my fear telling me will happen?" It's not uncommon for old memories of "what happened last time" to dictate what we believe will happen now. Write this down to recognize it's your past talking.

3. Notice that this is just a story you've made up in reaction to the fear. It hasn't happened yet. Can you see that you have a different choice of how to respond, if you stay awake to a different possibility that might unfold here and now?

4. Ask yourself, "What story do I want to write?" In other words, how would you like to see things turn out? Having this vision is important to helping you see another way. Hint: What would an ally do? Remember the Better Man Pledge and refer back to it if necessary.

5. Summon the courage to take the risk of leading from your heart. The Latin root of courage is *cor*, which means "heart." Be willing to tap into your own courage to step forward in a new way, knowing you might make a mistake. But that it's okay anyway.

6. Decide to take action. Actions you can take include admitting your fear to another person, asking for help (perhaps from your accountability buddy or a female mentor), and voicing that you don't know the answer.

You might also call someone's behavior out in a meeting, or invite other voices to be expressed. Decide on which one it will be and commit to following through.

Learning to Be With Sadness and Grief/Loss

One thing is for sure: COVID-19 put most everyone, if not everyone, in touch with loss. Loss of a loved one. A job. Connection. Loss of being able to experience our friends and family the way we are accustomed to. Most of us don't take a grief class in school; it's usually the "school of life" that has us learn and experience loss, and the accompanying stages that come with grief.

In my own life and in my work with men, I've found that being with sadness is a body of work that men need to learn most. We all carry with us past losses from our upbringing that still reside, unexperienced, in our bodies. And in the context of being a leader and ally, it's extremely important that you can connect to and experience your own sadness and grief when it shows up.

Why? Because if you don't, it will remain buried—until an unsuspecting life event comes along and triggers you. And instead of you experiencing and showing your true feelings, anger will rue the day. This is what we saw with Jim.

Second, you will be ill-equipped to deal with these same emotions when others around you experience them. Part of being an ally requires that you be empathetic. *The people with whom you work and lead, especially women and marginalized folks, live with loss, sadness, and grief all the time. You will need to be grounded in understanding what's true for them so that you can be a supportive ally and leader.* That's why it's so important that you start with *you.* I have an exercise for you that I use myself and that I offer to my coaching clients.

Think back to chapter three's exercise for connecting to your feelings.

Sadness/grief/loss release: "To feel is to heal"

When I first started to learn about and experience my own sadness, I began to realize the relief and release I would feel after a good cry. Even if it was brief, I felt good afterward. As for grief and loss, I recognized that they were much stronger and more complex and required a bit more thought—and willingness—to feel.

In fact, I actually was afraid of experiencing them, that they were too strong and I would be consumed by feeling them. Many men have shared similar fears. I want to tell you that despite these fears, you won't stop breathing or die from fully experiencing your sadness, grief, or loss. In fact, you will feel better and likely gain an insight or two.

I gained the insight that it's better to feel a little bit of sadness along the way or, as I invite you to consider, to take some of the air out of grief and loss by "unscrewing the lid a bit."

I think you will find that when you allow yourself to experience feelings of sadness, grief, and loss, they will not consume you—rather, you will feel somewhat lighter for having allowed them to be experienced. The energy it takes to stuff or ignore these emotions is not only wasted energy, but it increases the likelihood that these stuffed emotions will eat away at you internally or come out in the form of anger down the road.

My experiences and observations lead me to believe that a lot of men who haven't done a men's weekend or any kind of therapy may not even be aware of how much stress and internal tension is generated by shoving down feelings of grief/sadness/loss.

You may be wondering why I am going to this depth of explanation about this. As a man of multiple privileges, I've come to recognize that for me to be truly empathetic to others, to feel what they feel, I must experience my own emotions. This is what allows me to be there for others and advocate for them.

The goal of this exercise is to let out what's inside a little bit at a time, instead of it building up. Simply put, feeling this emotion gives it the release it's looking for. By experiencing it, you can support your own healing—which allows you to hold space for others.

There are several ways you can "unscrew the lid" and allow some sadness, loss, or grief to be experienced. One way is to go out in nature. Another is to find a place in your home where you can turn on some music. I'll walk you through both. This exercise is for you when you are amidst some loss, feeling sad, or grieving. This exercise is not about figuring out why you feel what you feel . . . it is just to give it some release.

In-nature release exercise

1. Locate a place outside where nobody is within earshot of you (you are going to make some noise).

2. Locate the feeling of sadness in your body. For example, you might notice a heaviness in your stomach or around your heart. Take a breath into it. This gives you the opportunity to experience the sadness by feeling it, which is far different than avoiding the feeling of it.

3. As you are feeling it, give it a sound. You can do this by answering, "If it had a sound, what would it be?" (It might sound like a whimper.) Imagine that you have your hand on a volume dial, and slowly raise the volume to a two or three.

4. Raise the volume of sound coming out of you. You may notice an instinct to cry.

5. Allow the sadness to express itself, and then you can stop.

6. Check in with yourself and see how you feel now.

For the musically inclined

One night during the pandemic, I was feeling down. I had just sat down to dinner with my wife and was fiddling with the Sonos app on my phone to turn on some music. She asked what I was doing, and I told her that I wanted to turn on some type of ballad so I could—and before I could say the word *feel*, I started to cry. Then she started to cry. It was cathartic. It felt GOOD.

I realized in that moment that something as simple as a melody can evoke the feelings of sadness one needs to experience. It inspires an emotion not unlike when you watch a movie and you tear up. This isn't that different. But it is intentional. In that moment, I realized this process could be replicated; I've shared it with several of my coaching clients and I offer it to you.

The opportunity to move spontaneously into an emotional release comes from your conscious choice to unscrew the lid a bit, allowing the sadness or grief that is asking to be experienced to move through you. In that spirit, you can try this version.

1. Choose a song/music genre/melody to listen to and pick a place where nobody is within earshot of you.

2. Turn on the tune and locate the feeling of sadness in your body. For example, you might notice a heaviness in your stomach or around your heart. Take a breath into it. This gives you the opportunity to experience the sadness by feeling it, which is far different than avoiding the feeling of it.

3. Breathe into that space in your body where you have located sadness.

4. You may notice an instinct to cry.

5. Allow the sadness to express itself, and then you can stop.
6. Check in with yourself and see how you feel now.

Congratulations: You've officially dealt with some pretty strong emotions. The simple process you just completed can be done multiple times as a way to change your pattern from stuffing emotions to releasing them. Again, this new and healthier approach to dealing with your emotions will not only pay off in your personal life but make you a better leader as well.

NEXT STOP: ACKNOWLEDGE AND UNDERSTAND YOUR PRIVILEGE

Privilege is a charged word for many people and therefore within companies. Mention white privilege, and white people get defensive and shut down. Mention it to companies, and they will likely ask that you substitute the word with "advantage."

Some people only have negative connotations for privilege and take it personally when they're identified as having some form of it. *My invitation is to consider this:* Privilege doesn't mean that there is anything wrong with us as men.

In her book *White Fragility*, Robin DiAngelo focuses on the challenges white people have when talking about racism. She defines "white fragility" as discomfort and defensiveness on the part of a white person when confronting racial inequality and injustice. I couldn't agree more.

It's tempting for people to interpret their privilege as meaning that they are bad people. Many white men in our current social and political climate often feel singled out and wrong, simply because they are white and male. The same is also true for white women.

This one word, *privilege*, can create feelings of guilt, anger, shame, and fear. Along with those feelings come the behaviors of defensiveness, denial, closing off, shutting down. While all these emotional reactions are valid, they don't contribute to the kind of leadership, community, and work environments where we all thrive for simply being who we are.

Similarly, when confronted by the inequality and injustice that women experience, many men are unsure of how to respond and manage their emotions. So, we often stay silent or sidestep the issues. This reality is also true for those with privilege(s) that people who belong to underrepresented groups do not have.

Privilege in a workplace context is only just beginning to be examined, and by few companies. The challenge is that privilege is deep-seated in our society, cultures, and history.

The journey of becoming an ally requires us to navigate privilege so that we can do three things:

> Seek to understand what privilege is and what it isn't
> Own our privilege for ourselves and understand its unexamined impact on others
> Choose how and when to use our privilege

Allow me to illustrate why this part of the journey is so imperative. Imagine that you are riding a bike, and a tailwind is blowing behind you, making it easier to pedal and go forward.

Now, imagine riding the same bike with a headwind that's making it harder, requiring you to put in more effort than the people who ride bikes with no headwind. In both instances, neither party has control over the winds. The tailwind is akin to privilege. It's not something we earn, yet it can benefit us immensely.

As a retired road bike racer, I learned that by pedaling to get in front of a rider, I could reduce their effort to go the same speed as I am going by 30 percent. Now that I am aware of my advantage, I can occasionally "ride in front" and use my strength to support another rider, allowing them to get ahead more easily without having to spend "extra" energy to travel the same distance. In the end, both cyclists advance further because they share the responsibility of riding "in front"—making more mutual progress, faster.

If we extend this analogy to privilege and oppression, we can use our privilege to offer alliance and support the progress of people who have been riding in headwinds their whole life. Everyone wins.

If we, as allies, are going to take responsibility for our role in making gender equality a reality, then we must do the internal work that will make us better leaders. That's what I'm here to guide you through. This all begins with gaining a true understanding of privilege so we can then learn how to use it for the good of others.

What Privilege Is (and Isn't)

Privilege is "an advantage that only one person or group of people has." Groups are advantaged based on a variety of factors: age, education level, ability/disability, ethnic or racial background, gender, sexual orientation, religion, social class, and more.

People of privilege may avoid some issues, roadblocks, glass ceilings, and slights that underprivileged people don't. Privileged people move through life more easily and safely than people who face more obstacles along the same path.

Everyone, in one way or another, has privilege. Some of us have many privileges. Some privileges are gained and others are accidents of birth. For me, I was born male and white, which simply comes with certain privileges that I don't have to work for. For others, such as women, people of color, and people who belong to other underrepresented groups, more effort is often required to obtain the same benefits that someone such as me has.

Earned vs. Unearned Privilege

Many kinds of privilege are accidents of birth over which you have no choice. For me, they are: whiteness, maleness, US citizenship, heterosexuality, and being cisgender (i.e., being the gender you are assigned at birth). At six-three, I even have "tall guy" privileges. And I am fine owning all of these because I recognize they don't mean anything about me personally, good or bad.

The real work for us lies in understanding how our unexamined privilege affects people other than ourselves. If I don't experience a certain form of oppression due to my gender and skin color, I have a privilege that an oppressed group does not. For example, when I walk into a room or down the street, in all likelihood I will be accepted at both a conscious and unconscious level. If I speak up or ask a question at a networking event amongst peers, they will most likely listen. Now, if I were a woman, man of color, or belonged to another disprivileged group, it's likely that I wouldn't be granted the same treatment.

Allies and inclusionary leaders who are intent on bettering themselves must acknowledge the existence of privilege, without shame. With the intention that once you are aware of and accept you have it in one or more modes of being, you can make good choices about what to do with it to support others. Let's take a deeper look at this often misunderstood and charged word.

When Privilege Goes Unchecked

To be blind to your own privilege only adds to the burden carried by most people who belong to marginalized groups. Acting from a place of unawareness and then apologizing for it later is similarly unhelpful—even if the apology comes from a place of good intentions. To illustrate, let's imagine you are a man in a meeting dominated by men with few or one woman. If, in this meeting, men are dominating the conversation—or worse, using negative language to suppress a woman's voice—it is up to you as an ally to stop and make the space welcoming for her contribution.

The opportunity you have, as a man among men, to be a good leader is a privilege women don't have. So, to not use it and to stay silent instead is a classic example of privilege unchecked. This has a very real and negative impact on others.

In a recent study featured in the university's *Y Magazine*, Brigham Young University's political science professor Jessica R. Preece and her colleagues examined the female experience in a collegiate accounting program. In this program, men were the majority, but women had higher GPAs and more leadership experience than the men.

The group explored what goes on in the meeting room when there is only one woman amongst men. What they found was a correlation between gender composition and negative interruptions. When one woman is meeting with four men, 70 percent of the interruptions she receives from men are negative. Wow! Not surprisingly, they found that when four women are in the room, only 20 percent of men's interruptions of women are negative. To quote the study, "When women have the majority in the room, 'men undergo a drastic change. They become far less aggressive.'"

By allowing this type of behavior, men lose out—because potentially good ideas and different perspectives stop being brought forward. I invite you to use your privilege to uplift and include the voices and contributions of others.

With this concept of privilege squarely in front of you, you can now begin to "own" it so that it doesn't own you.

Use Privilege for Good: A Simple Process

As people aspiring to be allies and inclusive leaders, it's important that we seek to acknowledge privilege to better understand how to support others. Even more powerful is how we use this privilege to "decenter" the attention on us and center the attention on other people who don't have the same privileges.

Humanize and appreciate your privilege

All humans, in one way or another, have some sort of privilege, whether earned or due to random circumstances of birth. To humanize privilege requires a fundamental recognition that having privilege doesn't mean anything is wrong with us. This makes it easier to own our privilege(s). Additionally, being able to appreciate your privilege sets you up to use it for the good of others.

To illustrate, I appreciate the fact that because I am a cisgender, white, heterosexual man, my unearned privileges afford me safety, recognition, and acceptance by the culturally dominant group (men). I can gain access more easily to conversations, opportunities, and more. I recognize that those who don't present like me have a much harder time. Knowing this, I want to use it for the good of others.

Think about what privileges you might have that you had no choice over (unearned privileges). Were you born male? Do you identify as heterosexual? Are you able-bodied? Were you born into wealth? These are just a few. You can continue this inquiry by asking yourself what privileges have been bestowed upon you that give you advantages that others may not have. Take a moment to write them down.

What are your unearned and earned privileges that you can appreciate? **Take a moment to reflect and write them down.** Notice if any feelings/judgments arise.

Model the behavior of owning privilege in front of others

When I lead workshops or do keynotes, one of the first things I do is own who I am as a man, acknowledging my privileges in front of everyone. This means that I name them. I say, for example, "I have privilege as a cisgender, white, heterosexual man." I even often say, "I have the tall guy's privilege because I'm six-three!" This sends the message to others that I am aware of them and myself in relation to them. This sets the tone for safety (theirs) in the environment.

An additional reason I model my behavior for other men to see is so that they, too, can begin to flex their own muscles of awareness. Inclusionary leaders who open up a dialogue and exploration around privilege in a group setting can identify themselves and encourage others to do the same.

It's unlikely that your line of work is like mine, so the opportunity to stand in front of your team or in a meeting to verbally own your privileges is unlikely and wouldn't necessarily serve a purpose.

However, owning your privileges in one-on-one conversations with men can have an impact that supports them in doing the same. Secondly, what is more important than owning them (which is necessary) is what you do with them once you've owned them.

Use the power of choice: an exercise

Once you become aware of your privilege and are able to own it without any negative self-judgment, you can arrive at a place of choice. This is where you get to decide how to use your privilege in order to support and advance others.

I'm going to walk you through several questions that will help you make a plan for your privilege.

Please grab a notebook and jot down your answers. Writing them out is a way of committing to taking action on our ideas.

Do I recognize the tacit rights, immunities, or benefits I enjoy by virtue of my gender, race, age, religion, education, and/or physical abilities? In the "humanize and appreciate my privilege" section above, you spent some time listing privileges that you have earned and those that were bestowed upon you at birth (unearned privilege).

The intention of asking this question is simply to support your ability to empathize with those who don't, and possibly can't ever, obtain these privileges. When I become aware of all the advantages bestowed upon me simply because I am a white, middle-aged male, able-bodied, with a post-college graduate degree, it helps me to imagine others who don't have these advantages. This sets me up to then ask, "What do I want to do with my privileges?"

〈〈 〉〉

What do I want to do with my privileges?
This is a personal choice and obviously this will be different for every person. For me personally, what I most want to do with my privilege is to use it for good, for the sake of others' inclusion and advancement.

Take a few moments to tune into what you'd like to do with the privilege you have.
Sometimes, the first thing that comes to mind is what you're seeking at a gut, or instinctual, level. Go with it.

Make a note of what you desire to do with your privilege.

It can be helpful to ask yourself why you are doing this work and then think backwards from there. For example, explore why you may want to change the culture at work. Once you have identified this, you can figure out the best action in terms of what to do with your privilege in order to achieve that.

《 》

What can I do with my privileges?

Each person can use privilege in numerous ways. For example, you can set up networking events that include women and underrepresented people. You might offer someone else the opportunity to take the lead on an initiative. Perhaps you will use your position and privilege to insist on a more diverse slate of candidates for a project. And, of utmost importance, you can speak about your privilege in front of others, modeling for them what using privilege for good looks like.

Write down a few ideas of what you can do with your privilege.

Here's an example. As a white male leader, I can decenter myself by centering another person, which means allowing their voice to be primary. I can do this in meetings, group settings, and in workshops. As the founder of the Better Man Conference, I routinely invite others who don't look like me and have different life experiences to deliver valuable learning experiences.

《 》

What is my responsibility as a person with privileges?
It is the responsibility of us all to use what is available to us in terms of power, position, and privileges. In so doing, we help to level the playing field and include all voices "at the table." Being a bystander is not an option once we understand privilege.

When we speak up and out, we create psychological safety for others to be themselves and to contribute their perspectives unencumbered. Psychological safety is non-negotiable for leaders who want to support inclusion. By setting the tone and holding others responsible for an environment where everyone has a voice, people feel a sense of belonging and bring their best selves to work.

Spend a few minutes deciding what your responsibility is as a person who may have privileges that others around you do not. Write them down.
Now that you've gotten in touch with your privilege and understand several ways in which you can use it for good, commit to walking the walk.

Write a few sentences in the form of action statements that bring together your answers from the above questions.
An example of one I might write: "I commit to inviting a diverse panel of speakers to the next workshop, which will include three people with life experiences and perspectives that are most unlike my own."

> The more specific you are, the more likely you will
> follow through. And follow-through—not ideas—is
> what makes us great allies.

It's important that you take a moment to reflect on the introspective journey you've taken thus far with respect to acknowledging your stuff. Awareness is the most important step in the
Ally's Journey, as it sets the stage for all subsequent steps.

A QUICK REVIEW
OF WHAT YOU'VE ACCOMPLISHED

I've introduced you to a lot of material in support of acknowledging your stuff. A LOT.

You've had an opportunity to learn from a real story about a
man who decided to put himself on the journey to becoming an
inclusive leader. His story demonstrated the potential influences
that your father (or father equivalent) may have exerted in shaping
your individual man box. You examined your own behaviors; this
is key, because knowing what drives your behavior allows you to
make changes to the unhealthy ones.

You went deep into your emotions and learned some techniques to bring more awareness to and release previously inexpe-
rienced emotions. This is extremely important as it contributes
to your own emotional literacy. It makes it possible to respond
instead of react, and to empathize.

You learned what privilege is, what it isn't, what happens if it
remains unexamined, and how to appreciate privilege as opposed
to making it a bad thing. All of this allowed you to consciously

consider and commit to how you can use your privilege for good to support others.

Much of this chapter is about what I call "Conscious Head." The next chapter will explore Conscious Heart. Ultimately, the work of being an ally and inclusive leader requires a Conscious Partnership of the Head and Heart. It is time for you to journey to your heart!

Before you go, let's look at the key lessons you've learned.

> ## > Key Lessons

Step one of the Ally's Journey is about bringing awareness to what drives your behavior, which requires you to "acknowledge your stuff." By doing so, you can make changes to your behavior.

You learned that there are several unwritten but adhered to rules of what it means to be a real man that don't serve you or others.

We discussed how your father or father figure equivalents can play a significant role in influencing your behavior when it comes to being a man, how you treat a woman, and how you emotionally express yourself.

You brought awareness and connected to your emotions of fear, sadness, anger, and shame to support your emotional literacy.

Lastly, you learned that privilege is something you both earn and have bestowed upon you by birth. Unexamined, it can harm others; examined, you can choose to use it for good.

Ready for the next step?

< CHAPTER FIVE >

STEP TWO
OF THE ALLY'S JOURNEY

Listen, Really

The second step of being an ally and inclusive leader is all about listening, arguably the most important aspect of communication. What may be new for many of you is where to listen from: the heart.

As I shared with you in a story in chapter one, the newsroom men had the opportunity to listen to the experiences of the women with whom they worked. When we went around the room, *most, if not all, of the men wanted to do something because of what they heard. It is because they felt empathy.* This is what happens when the experience of others is illuminated. Empathetic listening activated the men to want to take action.

Empathetic listening is the most challenging form of listening and occurs when we try to understand or experience what a speaker is thinking or feeling. It's distinct from sympathetic listening; while the word empathy means to "feel into" or "feel with" another person, sympathy means to "feel for" someone. Sympathy is generally more self-oriented and distant than empathy.

< 103 >

As a man, I wasn't trained to listen empathetically, nor did I see someone model it. I learned it.

Empathetic listening helps maintain interpersonal relationships, both at work and home. In order for a monologue to become dialogue, people commit to civility and to being open-minded to a degree that allows them to be empathetic while still believing in and advocating for their own position. Remember your Better Man Pledge? This is one of the places where your commitment can be realized.

The newsroom men wanted to better understand their female colleagues' experiences and were intent on improving their culture and their peers' day-to-day work life. These men made the journey to their hearts—from which they were listening, rather than from their heads. Listening from the head will be explored in this chapter in further detail below.

As a white heterosexual male, I enjoy a variety of privileges that shield me from the vast variety of microaggressions experienced regularly by women and marginalized folks. As an ally and inclusionary leader, one way I can connect and empathize with them is to listen, from a place of curiosity, to their experiences. And it wasn't always this way. It required some work on my part.

Different Situations Require Different Types of Listening

Listening serves many purposes. As leaders, the type of listening we engage in affects our communication and how others respond to us. For example, when we listen to empathize with others, our communication will likely be supportive and open—which will then lead the other person to feel "heard" and supported, and hopefully to view the interaction positively.

Women colleagues and marginalized folks need this from you. This creates psychological safety for them that enables them to bring their whole selves to work. Inevitably, when you are able to accomplish this, it shines the light on you as a true ally and inclusive leader.

Implications of Listening for Relationships, at Home and at Work

You shouldn't underestimate the power of listening to make someone else feel better and open your perceptual field to new sources of information. Empathetic listening can help you expand your social awareness by learning from other people's experiences and taking on different perspectives.

Moments of Stress and Conflict

During times of conflict, emotional support in the form of empathetic listening and validation can help relational partners successfully manage common relationship stressors that may have otherwise led a partnership to deteriorate. When you reflect back to the person that you are listening, so that you recognize their feelings and hear their opinion, and that their feelings and opinions are worthwhile, you are validating them. This doesn't mean you agree with them.

Are Men and Women Different?

Most men have not been conditioned or trained to listen with empathy and compassion. This doesn't mean that you can't. Much of the research on gender differences and communication has been influenced by gender stereotypes and falsely credits biological differences.

More recent research has found that people communicate in ways that conform to gender stereotypes in some situations but not in others, which shows that your communication is more influenced by societal expectations than by innate or gendered "hardwiring." For example, through socialization, men are generally discouraged from expressing emotions in public. This is the man box in action.

The biggest difference between men and women and their styles of communication boils down to the fact that men and women view the purpose of conversations differently. Academic research on psychological gender differences has shown that while women use communication as a tool to enhance social connections and create relationships, men use language to exert dominance and achieve tangible outcomes. Women are, overall, more expressive, tentative, and polite in conversation, while men are more assertive and power-hungry.

My conclusion from this research is that we, as men, *can* approach our communication, listening, and our ability to lead inclusively from a different perspective. *Biology is not in the way, nor is it an excuse; rather, our ideology can allow us to reset our own personal context to become better allies and inclusive leaders.*

We often see the influence of gender stereotypes play out in the workplace. Let's consider the following story to get a better sense of what this looks like in action.

A STORY

Samantha had just been promoted to Vice President of Sales. Her mentor Ron had previously occupied this position and was now her direct report. He was to accompany and support her in an upcoming transition meeting. Ron had worked with Samantha to hone her presentation for the sales team. He also knew the team well.

Samantha and Ron walked into the room of all men. Most of the men made an effort to say hi to Ron; most merely exchanged glances with Samantha. She didn't exactly feel welcomed.

Samantha loaded her USB memory stick into the computer for her presentation. She looked around the room and announced that she was going to get started. All but two of her colleagues, Keith and Jack, sat down as they were finishing a conversation—there was no other acknowledgment of her request. "Come on, guys," she said once more, and they took their seats. She was starting to feel the familiar burden of exerting extra effort to get men's attention.

As she launched into her presentation, another member of the team, Justin, interrupted: "Can't you just move to the revenue projections?" Samantha responded that she would in due time. After a few more slides, when she launched into her sales strategy, Keith questioned her: "Do you really think that this will work with our customer base?" Samantha was starting to feel deflated.

As her presentation came to a close, Jack made a sexually derogatory comment about what she was wearing. Ron, just as he had the whole time, remained silent. Samantha asked if there were any questions; nobody answered. She grabbed her USB and walked out with a fake smile on her face—masking the intense humiliation, isolation, and frustration she was feeling on the inside.

Samantha did her best to assemble her thoughts, intent on having a conversation with Ron, who followed her out of the room and into the hall.

"I can't believe what just happened in there! That did not go well," Samantha said.

Ron's response? "What are you talking about? I thought it went fine."

Ron's comment only made it worse.

Samantha tried again: "Both Justin and Keith interrupted me and basically undermined me in front of the other guys. And what about the comment Jack made about my dress? YUCK!"

Ron responded, "That's just guys being guys. I thought you could handle it. You need to develop thicker skin if you are going to lead a bunch of guys. Otherwise they won't follow you."

At this point, Samantha started to feel dejected, not supported. She answered, "While all of this was going on, you just stood silent like the rest of them. You knew how important this meeting was, and you bailed on me. I'm out of here."

Instead of staying quiet because now *he was feeling uncomfortable*, Ron uttered, "I didn't mean for this to happen." Already halfway down the hall, Samantha didn't bother to respond.

Taking a Closer Look: What Happened?

In this story, a lot happened in a short period of time. Many of the microaggressions Samantha endured in the meeting will be addressed in step three of the Ally's Journey, taking responsibility. For the purposes of this chapter, there are numerous examples of what "listening from the head" looks like in action.

Listening from the head is characterized by:

> Preparation: Disagreement, Defending, and/or Defeating what the other person said
> Binary Thinking: Agree/Disagree, Win/Lose, Justify/Invalidate
> Confirmation Bias: Listening to confirm what you already believe to be true

In the meeting, the first instance of "listening from the head" occurred when Justin interrupted and asked the question, "Can't you just move to the revenue projections?" This is an example of *manterrupting*, which is the unnecessary interruption of a woman by a man (we will explore this concept in greater detail in chapter seven). This is an example of binary listening. It shows up as invalidating, not to mention disrespectful.

Interrupting a woman sends the message that what she has to say doesn't matter. When this happens repeatedly—which it will, until men break the pattern of behavior—women begin to change their behavior. The more you interrupt a woman, the less likely she will speak. The less a woman speaks, the less influence she is perceived to have. For her, this pattern typically results in limited upward mobility and advancement. The organization or company misses her valuable input and contributions. Eventually, she leaves the company. Now, your bottom line is impacted.

The second instance of listening from the head occurred after Justin's interruption opened the door for Keith to question her: "Do you really think that this will work with our customer base?" This is an example of *defeatist listening*, when, rather than truly listening with curiosity, the listener prepares to defeat, defend, or disagree with what the other person says.

Listening from the head doesn't support Samantha; instead, it lessens what she is trying to present. Justin and Keith's non-supportive listening is already wearing Samantha down. Put yourself in Samantha's shoes: Would you feel supported or attacked? What would you do if this happened to you? How would it make you feel?

The third listening from the head infraction occurred when Ron and Samantha spoke after the meeting. Ron missed an opportunity to listen from the heart that instead led him to make several mistakes.

Ron's first mistake was when Samantha expressed her frustration about what happened. Ron's dismissive reply—"What are you talking about? I thought it went fine"—was an example of *binary listening*, when Ron disagreed with what Samantha was sharing. Ron, also without knowing it, *minimized her experience*. He did not reflect back to Samantha that he recognized her feelings and heard her opinion, and that her feelings and opinions were worthwhile, and so he *did not validate her.*

Samantha needed to be heard and empathized with, not disagreed with. The impact here is that Samantha doesn't feel supported by Ron; in her mind, he is just like the rest of them. This whole experience was humiliating and now isolating, too, because it's her against them.

Ron made another listening from the head mistake when Samantha brought up Justin's interrupting, Keith's undermining, and Jack's sexually derogatory comment. Ron's reply—"That's just guys being guys"—was yet another example of binary listening from the head, a justification for man box behavior. Once again, Ron missed an opportunity to validate her experience. Samantha, as a result, is not being supported and feels even more isolated.

Ron's comment, "You need to develop thicker skin if you are going to lead a bunch of guys," lands like this: "You need to be more like a guy. Being a woman isn't okay." This is pretty close to putting the proverbial nail in the coffin. It's a twofold example of binary listening: invalidating her way of being and defeating her statement about her experience of the meeting.

Lastly, when Samantha called Ron out for being silent the whole time, his response— "I didn't mean for this to happen"— fell woefully short. *Intent versus impact* is an important concept to understand when seeking to become an ally. When someone shares with you that something you did or said landed in a way that was hurtful to them, your response of, "I didn't mean for that to happen," not only avoids responsibility but additionally minimizes the person's experience. Not the best move, if you want to be an ally.

Now, we are going to spend some time learning about listening from the heart.

FROM THE HEART: LISTENING WITH EMPATHY AND COMPASSION

Listening with empathy and compassion is a very important step in the Ally's Journey. Despite man box influences, fatherly influences, and societal enforcement of gender stereotypes, men can learn to listen with empathy and compassion—I know because I have learned how. There is one huge difference between listening from the head rather than from the heart. The former causes further negative impact and encourages disconnection; the latter evokes empathy, understanding, and connection, which creates allies in action.

Listening from the heart is characterized by:

> **Growth Mindset:** Listening to learn something you don't already know
> **Empathy:** Understanding the experiences and resulting feelings of the speaker
> **Compassion:** Genuine interest in the speaker's concerns, perspectives, and ideas
> **Generosity:** Listening with curiosity about the speaker's point of view without seeking agreement

Employing these ways of listening first requires self-awareness. In the previous chapter, you acknowledged your stuff—examining emotions, privilege, man box rules, and fatherly influences. You will be well served by keeping what you learned about yourself front-of-mind, because "your stuff" *can influence how you listen.* Staying awake to this possibility paves the way for you to listen actively, supporting your intention to be an empathetic listener.

Tom Bruneau, a prominent scholar of empathetic listening, describes it this way: "Empathetic listening is to be respectful of the dignity of others. Empathetic listening is a caring, a love of the wisdom to be found in others whoever they may be." This type of listening is more philosophical than the other types. It requires that we be open to subjectivity and that we engage in it because we genuinely see it as worthwhile.

Active Listening Plus Empathetic Listening

Combining active and empathetic listening leads to active-empathetic listening. During active-empathetic listening, a listener becomes actively and emotionally involved in an interaction. It is conscious on the part of the listener and it is perceived by the speaker.

When you commit as an ally and inclusive leader to active and empathetic listening, women and people who belong to marginalized groups will feel supported, understood, and valued. They will follow you and bring their full contribution.

TRAINING SECTION

This training section offers some techniques to guide you in how to listen. Additionally, I have a few simple assignments to develop your listening skills in support of your empathy building.

Here are a few suggested techniques you can use.

LISTEN TO WHAT'S GOING ON INSIDE OF YOU— LEARNING TO ACCEPT FEEDBACK EXERCISE

The journey of becoming an ally and inclusive leader will most certainly include instances of you saying or doing the wrong thing—and it results in impacting another, despite your intent.

Knowing this and being willing to "keep going" despite it is the hallmark of what it means to be an ally and inclusive leader. It's important to remember your humanness: We all make mistakes. More than anything else, it's what you do *after* the mistake that says the most about you. One heart-based leadership principle, accountability, comes to mind.

Accountability is all about taking responsibility for one's words, actions, choices, and their consequences, intended or not. What I want you to consider here, in the context of listening, is that accountability and emotional literacy work together. Allow me to illustrate: As a heart-based leader who strives to be accountable for your words and actions, you will have the ability to actively listen to your emotions, acknowledging and experiencing them, so you can respond instead of react.

There will be times when a woman or person who belongs to a marginalized group gives you feedback about how what you said or did landed. For now, it's most important to focus on what feelings/emotions that brings up **for you.** You might feel fear, anger, shame, guilt, or even sadness. Don't gloss over these feelings. Acknowledge them and "take a beat" (explained below).

Accepting Feedback Like an Ally (AFLA)

When someone offers you feedback regarding your behavior, consider AFLA.

1. Consider that the feedback given to you is *supportive* and can contribute to your growth.

2. *Remember* that this is their experience, that they have taken some risk to be vulnerable.

3. Upon hearing the feedback, *notice the feelings* that come up inside you.

4. Notice if you want to *defend, disagree, or offer an explanation.* You are still in listening mode, so remember to stay silent.

5. Consider that the very thing you want to defend, disagree, or explain is perhaps the *very thing you need to look at and get support around.*

6. Say, "Thank you. I'm sorry, and I will work on this."

In the next chapter, I will explore this deeply and offer more tools to support your accountability as an ally and inclusive leader when you misstep.

Supportive, Active-Listening Techniques

Take a look at each of these and give them a try. They will be useful in the assignment I give you at the end of this training section.

Take a beat

As a listener, build on your emotional literacy by noticing your feelings in the moment. With respect to AFLA, recall that on hearing feedback about your behavior, you can "take a beat"— that is, breathe, experience your emotion, and respond instead of react. This technique is especially helpful when receiving feedback from someone who has been affected by your words or actions.

Suspend your judgment of the other person (or what they are saying)

To be a better empathetic listener, you need to suspend—or at least attempt to suppress—your judgment of the other person or their message, so you can fully attend to both them and their words. Assume positive intent. This means being open to the possibility that they are sharing this with you to help you grow, as opposed to criticizing you. This will support you in quieting your mind while you listen.

Paraphrase their words

Paraphrasing is an important part of empathetic listening, because it helps you put the other person's words into your frame of experience without making it about you.

In addition, speaking someone else's words in our own voice can help evoke within us the feelings experienced by the other person while saying them. Active-empathetic listening is more than echoing back verbal messages.

Example: Speaker: "I'm having a hard time communicating with Bill and I don't know what's going on."

Paraphrased reply: "It sounds like you're frustrated that you and Bill aren't getting along." This results in the speaker feeling heard.

Mirror their nonverbal signals

We can also engage in mirroring, which refers to a listener's replication of a speaker's nonverbal signals.

Example: Adopt a posture and tone similar to the person speaking to you in order to build rapport and project empathy.

Seek to understand by asking questions

Questions that ask for elaboration act as "verbal door openers." Inviting someone to speak more and then validating their speech through active listening cues can help a person feel "listened to." The impact on the other person is that they feel seen and included.

Example: "Can you say more about that?" "Tell me more."

Note: Paraphrasing and questioning are useful techniques for empathetic listening because they allow you to respond to a speaker without taking "the floor," or the attention, away for long.

Resist the temptation to tell your story or give unsolicited advice

I've found that paraphrasing and asking questions are also useful techniques when I feel tempted to share my own stories and experiences, rather than maintaining my listening role. Although it is easier (and tempting) for me to slip into an advisory mode—saying things like, "Well, if I were you . . ."—it is incumbent upon you (and me) to resist the temptation.

Telling your story makes it about you; not telling your story keeps the focus on them and fosters connection and trust.

A Simple Assignment

As part of your development as an ally and inclusive leader, this exercise encourages you to actively presence the experiences of women by asking them a few questions. Consider this an empathy-building exercise.

1. Identify a woman you know, who either works in your company or is a colleague of yours. Also consider a woman you may have a personal relationship with.
2. Share with her that you are an ally in training and that you would like to ask a few questions that support your active learning as an ally.
3. Ask one or all of the questions below.
4. *What is it like for you as a woman to work here?*

5. *What have you or other women been trying to tell the company that we haven't heard?*

6. *What do you want from men in the company?*

7. Listen empathetically (use the tips in the supportive, active-listening techniques section).

8. Notice what goes on inside of you (refer to AFLA).

A QUICK REVIEW
OF WHAT YOU'VE ACCOMPLISHED

Who said listening was easy? You have a lot to feel good about, with the progress you have made in this chapter. Yes, I said "feel!"

In this chapter, you gained an understanding of empathetic listening. You learned the critical importance of empathetic listening to being an ally and inclusive leader. The path to becoming an ally and inclusive leader will have instances where people share with you their experiences, possibly because of what you said or did. Or they might share what someone else said or did. Regardless, shifting from your conditioned way of listening—"from the head"—to "listening from the heart" is a skill you will most certainly need.

These active and empathetic listening skills will support you as you build relationships, improve your leadership and receive feedback, and diversify your own empathy-building skills for when you go into action as an ally.

You also learned that our communications as people are more influenced by societal expectations than biology, and that most men have not been conditioned to listen with empathy and compassion. This is courtesy of the man box influences. Though men may be from Mars and women from Venus, we can *all* listen with empathy and compassion.

Lastly, I gave you an assignment to make real these listening techniques by inviting you to have a few conversations with women you know. This is important for the simple reason that putting your intentions into actions is what will develop your empathy skills; starting with someone you know is always a good idea.

Remember, heart-based listening skills can be learned. They require awareness of your old patterns of listening behavior, and practice to break out of those patterns. Good job!

In the next chapter, we will build upon what you have learned thus far, so that you may step into accountability (a heart-based leadership principle) as an ally and leader. Taking responsibility for the impact of your behaviors and language—which are often influenced by unexamined privilege(s), biases, and man box rules—is the third step of the Ally's Journey. We will examine impact versus intent and equip you with some tools to "take responsibility."

Before you go, let's look at the key lessons you've learned.

> ### > Key Lessons

The ability to listen, really, is a game changer. It can transform how you communicate, which often results in ally-like behaviors, better relationships, and quality leadership.

> Most men have not been conditioned or trained to listen with empathy and compassion—it's societal expectations, not biology, that are behind this untrained skill.

> Listening from the head looks like defending, defeating, invalidating, and justifying your original words or actions when receiving feedback from another person. It negatively impacts the person

speaking, fostering disconnection from the listener.

> Listening from the heart—as evidenced by a growth mindset, empathy, compassion, and generosity—evokes empathy, understanding, and connection. It leads to allies in action.

> When you, as an ally and inclusive leader, commit to active and empathetic listening, women and people who belong to marginalized groups will feel supported, understood, and valued.

A critical part of listening includes listening to what is going on inside of you, especially when you receive feedback.

< CHAPTER SIX >

STEP THREE
OF THE ALLY'S JOURNEY

Take Responsibility

I imagine that it's quite easy to read the title of this chapter and feel a bit triggered, or like you've been accused of being part of the problem. You might even be wondering, "What problem?" That's okay!

Companies that commit to creating a true sense of belonging in their cultures know the benefits, and don't frame their diversity and inclusion efforts as "fixing a problem." They see diversity and inclusion efforts as a means of driving true business value. Smart companies know (and are learning) that there must also be a commitment to include men in their efforts. These companies are among the first to take responsibility for being part of the solution.

Meeting men where they are—and stressing the importance of the role they must play, as the overrepresented majority, in being part of the solution of equity, equality, and inclusion—is of paramount importance. These companies are all about finding and committing to a solution.

< 121 >

To all the men reading this chapter, I offer a positive way to contextually view your path to allyship: as a means to be part of the movement . . . or part of the solution of equity, equality, and inclusion. You are only "part of the problem" if you stay silent, neglect to use your privilege for the good of others, and continue allowing unexamined influences like bias, man box rules, and early male figures in your life to drive your behavior and negatively impact others.

As a man and leader, I take responsibility for the impact of my words, choices, and actions, intended or not—that is the definition I use for accountability in all areas of my life and leadership. There was a time when I couldn't truly appreciate what accountability had to do with me, what it looked like in action, and what it took to make the ongoing commitment of holding myself to account.

I now know that part of becoming a better man, on my way to being an ally and inclusive leader, requires reframing. Instead of focusing on the problem, I focus on the opportunity as well as the responsibility.

So, I invite you to sit with the questions: "What is the opportunity for you, as a man, to be part of the solution? How may it benefit you? Others? Your company?" Upon answering these questions, are you willing to take responsibility?

Sometimes it takes a difficult learning experience like making several mistakes to inform you how to do things the right way.

In order to truly appreciate this important step of the Ally's Journey, it's imperative that I give you the opportunity to see what typical ally behavior and its impacts look like in action, so as to better appreciate the experiences of others. As you have learned (and hopefully as a result of your assignment in chapter five), when you hear about women's experiences, your higher self wants to act, to do the right thing, and be the man you are capable of being.

Let's take a look at the following story.

A LEARNING EXPERIENCE

At the 2020 East Coast Better Man Conference, we decided to bring before the audience a senior male leader who was willing to authentically share his story so that other men in attendance could learn and eventually emulate what they saw. When I asked my diversity liaison at a Fortune 50 company that was one of our sponsors if she knew of such a man, in no less than five seconds, she said, "I know just the guy!" I told her that having a coaching conversation with him was going to play a very important role—not just at the conference, but internally, when it came to activating other men.

The plan was to have a fireside chat with this individual, an SVP from a Fortune 50 company, at the Better Man Conference. To prepare for the event, I set up a call with Jerry, a white man, to learn about his story.

During our call, I emphasized the importance of showing up and telling a story that would model "healthy masculinity" for other men at his company, as well as the male attendees, to emulate. I shared with him the power and necessity of being vulnerable, owning his mistakes and their impact, acknowledging his feelings, and showing his humanness—in front of other men. I also stressed the importance of him being accountable and taking responsibility for the impact of his actions.

At the conference, Jerry shared with me and the audience that Stacey, a woman of color who had previously reported to him, decided to leave the company without any warning. Stacey was a talented employee with lots of potential. Jerry had recently assigned her to work under another male leader in a parallel division, without having a conversation with her about it.

When she gave notice, Jerry asked for an opportunity to speak to her so he could better understand why she was leaving. Stacey informed him of the difficulty she was experiencing with her direct report, who was a white man. Not only was there no rapport with him, but she routinely was the recipient of his, and other men's, microaggressive behaviors; it was a difficult no-win situation for her. She described it as a hostile environment. There was no opening for Stacey to discuss this or remedy it, and she concluded it was impossible for her to have success with this guy. When she looked around for an ally (by her definition) and did not have one, she decided to leave the company.

Jerry asked Stacey, "Why didn't you reach out to me?"

Stacey's reply was telling: "I didn't feel supported by you, and it's been my experience that you weren't available to me and it left me with the impression that you didn't stand for my success." She went on to say that the impact of Joe's reassignment was that she thought he didn't value her. She asked, "Why would you assume that, as a woman of color, I would reach back out to you after you reassigned me to another white male leader?"

Jerry shared his initial response to her: *He thought he was helping Stacey by assigning her to another division and direct report to give her more experience.*

This was not how it felt to her. Stacey felt she had no other choice but to leave, in large part because there was no foundation of mutual trust and safety that a woman of color like herself needed from a white male leader. I knew this was hard for Jerry to hear. So, I didn't waste the opportunity.

I asked point-blank: "When you heard this, how did it make you feel?" On impulse, Jerry replied, "I felt *angry* at myself. I felt *guilty* and a bit of *shame* for my part in her experience."

He went on to share, humbly and matter-of-factly, that he took this experience as a learning opportunity and put himself on the path of becoming a better inclusive leader and ally. Jerry has since attended women's leadership events, worked on understanding his bias and privilege, and stepped into curiosity about the experiences of others. He also shared with me that there would be no more room for the toxic behaviors that men often exhibit in his organization.

Taking a Closer Look: What Happened?

This story is an example of many concepts: accountability (or lack thereof), unexamined privilege, man box behaviors, listening from the head, and intention without regard to impact.

The good news is that this is also a story of a man exemplifying step three of the Ally's Journey: holding himself accountable, listening from the heart, examining his privilege and making a choice to use it, and committing to move forward into action—and following through. Jerry also models how a man unwilling to tolerate the toxic behavior of other men can show up.

Lack of accountability

Senior leaders must be accountable for how their choices, decisions, language, and actions consequently affect others, in ways intended or not. Jerry made a unilateral decision to transfer Stacey; when it was brought to his attention that she was leaving, he missed his opportunity to take accountability for his choice and its consequences. Instead, he made a series of typical missteps that I have highlighted below.

Unexamined privilege

When Jerry assigned Stacey to work with another white male leader, his unexamined white male privilege was running the show. It didn't occur to him what it might be like for a woman of color working with, and for, predominantly white men in leadership. Remember: Privilege is invisible to those who have it. As white men, we see what we are accustomed to seeing, not necessarily through the lens of another person who doesn't identify as male and white.

Although Jerry can never know what it's like to be a woman of color, by examining his own privilege (step one of the Ally's Journey), he could have come to understand and appreciate how much more difficult it is—effort wise—for a woman (especially a woman of color) to be accepted, supported, and to thrive among a majority of white male leaders.

Now, imagine that most of the men at the Fortune 50 company have not examined their biases and privileges. It's not difficult to comprehend the repeated impact on someone like Stacey, and how this may very well be a hostile environment.

It didn't occur to Jerry how, as a white man amid many white male leaders, transferring Stacey to another white male leader might challenge her. Had Jerry been aware of the possibility of this in his own organization, he could have used his privilege and the power and responsibility that comes with it to provide cover for Stacey.

Inclusionary leaders have an opportunity to be an **advocate** by pushing (encouraging), promoting (in your network), and protecting (providing cover) on behalf of a woman. This concept is known as sponsorship, and it will be discussed in more detail in chapter seven.

Man box rule: "Men make the decisions"

Jerry erred when he decided that an assignment to another division might be good for Stacey without getting her input. One of the man box rules, "men make the decisions," is evident here. Jerry deciding what's best for Stacey is not unlike a male leader deciding that, because a woman colleague has kids, she wouldn't want to accept a promotion that requires travel. The impact that lands on the woman is that the man believes she is incapable of making this decision on her own. It doesn't matter what you might believe or assume; give her the chance to decide for herself. This is patriarchal leadership in action, and it is a microaggression.

Listening from the head: defending

After Stacey shared her experience, Jerry's binary listening from the head had him ask, "Why didn't you reach out to me?" Putting the onus on Stacey was a misstep because Stacey shared a difficult situation with Jerry—and *rather than empathize, Jerry defended.* The impact to Stacey here is that she doesn't feel heard, nor does she feel supported. This is another microaggression.

Intention versus impact: justifying with good intentions isn't good

When Stacey gave more reasons for not reaching out to him after he reassigned her, Jerry's attempt to explain the intention behind his decision to reassign her failed to acknowledge its impact. In fact, it had the net effect of invalidating her experience. This is yet another microaggression. As the microaggressions continue to build, Stacey starts to look for the exit.

What Jerry Did Well

As I mentioned previously, this is also a story of a man who began to exemplify step three of the Ally's Journey. What did Jerry do upon deeper reflection? He *acknowledged his feelings* of guilt. He *took responsibility for the impact of his unexamined privilege and bias* by learning about them so he wouldn't make the same mistake in the future. *He moved toward being part of the solution* by learning, attending women's events, and ultimately *setting the tone of zero tolerance* for toxic male behavior at his company.

What is important to point out here, is that Jerry answered a personal *wake-up call* of sorts. He *felt his emotions and acknowledged them publicly, which supports other men to follow his leadership by example.* He held himself *accountable* and resolved to hold other men accountable. He made a personal commitment.

Much of the Better Man Pledge is designed to encourage you to proactively put yourself on notice of what you need to do, so that you don't experience a wake-up call from which you need to work backward.

Missteps will occur along the way, that's for sure. I invite you to consider getting going sooner, jumpstarting your Ally's Journey without experiencing an event that negatively impacts another person.

Also worth pointing out is that Jerry took his responsibility as a leader seriously and was *vulnerable* in front of many men— sharing his feelings, his mistakes, and his learnings, so that other men could do the same. He showed the audience his *authenticity.* This moment was huge—not just for the men, but for the women witnessing Jerry and the men who were commenting on his story. It sparked possibility and *inclusivity.*

ACCOUNTABILITY 101

Accountability, as a principle of heart-based leadership, plays a critical role in your being an ally and inclusive leader. One of the Better Man Pledge commitments, "I will forever be an ally in training, recognizing that my bias and privilege may occasionally cause harm to another," requires accountability. It makes taking responsibility for your impact a reality.

I define accountability as taking responsibility for my words, choices, and actions and their consequences, intended or not. I invite you to learn this definition.

Again, becoming an ally and inclusionary leader will invite instances wherein despite your good intent, you will make mistakes—saying or doing something that is driven by your unexamined bias, privilege, or man box influences. It's part of the journey. Equally important is your vulnerability as an ally and leader. To be able to admit fault to another person in front of others, for the sake of others, is true power. Your willingness to be vulnerable makes it possible for others to be human, and to embark on their own respective journeys as allies and leaders.

One way you can begin to change your behavior is to understand *microaggressions* and their impact, which can be quite significant.

Microaggressions are how women and underrepresented people are affected in both social and working environments (remember that "death by a thousand cuts"?). When they happen, there is a responsibility and an opportunity to clean up your mistakes with the person you impacted as a result of your microaggression.

As an ally in training, and as a leader, these actions carry you from being part of the problem to being part of the solution.

This step of taking responsibility will help you recognize man-terrupting, manopolizing, mansplaining, and more. These behaviors and what they look like in the workplace will be addressed in the next chapter.

Accountability is often misunderstood and misused in life and business. I offer my perspectives on how accountability can support your leadership and allyship efforts.

First, *the only person who can hold you to account is you. It's your integrity that's on the line.* It's not your job to hold others accountable; rather, it's your responsibility to offer and provide support for their own accountability to themselves.

Second, *accountable leaders and allies take responsibility for what happens on their watch*. This is organizational accountability. In our story above, Jerry missed an opportunity to take responsibility for reassigning Stacey to a hostile environment, which led her to quit. He only asked, "Why didn't you call me?"

The positive effects of being accountable are mostly personal, in that your integrity is yours and yours alone. While sometimes difficult, it can be empowering to look at yourself in the mirror, remember your Better Man Pledge, and take accountability for your actions.

But your accountability also shows others around you how to stay out of the blame game. Your actions set the tone. At an organizational level, your commitment to accountability creates safety and trust for women and marginalized folks because they can rely on you.

A male inclusive leader who understands his privilege and the responsibility that comes with it would, from a place of curiosity, discuss with Stacey her goals and intentions. He would share his idea and seek her input.

FIRST THINGS FIRST:
DID THIS HAPPEN ON MY WATCH?

When someone shares with me the impact of something I said or did, I operate from a place of accountability: I acknowledge that this happened on **"my watch"** (because of something I said or did). I don't blame others, defend or rationalize, or speak to my intent.

This is where to start your accountability process. Did you say or do something that resulted in a microaggression against another person? Did this happen on your watch?

The temptation here is to avoid responsibility (often because of what you believe people will think about you), defend, or justify—none of which are becoming of an ally or inclusionary leader.

FROM ACCOUNTABILITY TO RESPONSIBILITY TO CLEAN UP

Once you've taken accountability for your words or actions, it's important that you take *personal responsibility for what you said* and its impact on the other person. This is where vulnerability, a heart-based leadership principle, is crucial. The ability to show oneself—your humanness, that you made a mistake and don't have all the answers—goes a long way in repairing your mistakes and restoring your relationships. Apologizing for your impact will be more well-received as a result. *Restoring the relationship is important,* because you can then commit to learning more and improving how you can interact and lead. Jerry didn't do this . . . initially. An exercise in the below training section will give you a road map for clean-up conversations.

The Importance of Examining White Male Privilege

You spent considerable time in chapter four, "Acknowledge Your Stuff," learning about and understanding privilege. You looked at privilege unchecked/unexamined in a meeting setting.

As a leader, oftentimes high-potential candidates in need of your leadership will come across your path. Sometimes, these candidates are women and folks of marginalized identity. Having an awareness of your white male privilege and the choices that come with it allows. you to see the field through the eyes of women and marginalized folks. Recognizing your advantages, and at the same time, the disadvantages of others in your organization will allow you to be an effective inclusionary leader and support your stepping into an advocacy role. With this recognition, there are choices you can consciously make to open doors and support their advancement. Sometimes, it will require you to protect them or "run air cover" for them.

The personal benefit is that you will have direct influence on the career well-being of another person, which will shine positively on your leadership. These individuals will respect your leadership and you will have the satisfaction of using your privilege for good, creating a culture of inclusion. Your actions will also serve as a model for other men in your organization.

She's an Adult—Let Her Decide For Herself

You learned in chapter one about the man box and its origins. In chapter four, you unpacked it to "Acknowledge Your Stuff." In our story above, you saw how unexamined influences can drive a well-intentioned leader to not include or consult a woman in a highly important decision that affects her career.

The important thing to stress here is that this type of leadership is patriarchal—the man makes the decision without discussing it with the woman. The unintended impact is that it sends the message that men know better, that the woman can't make these decisions for herself. When this happens repeatedly, it undermines a woman's confidence and ultimately her sense of well-being in an organization.

I invite you to contain your "good intentions" and instead step into listening from the heart by having a conversation with her about your ideas as they pertain to her career, asking for her input. If she is reluctant to step forward despite being highly qualified, this is a good opening to encourage her to step into the opportunity.

Everyone benefits from this approach. She has some control over her career trajectory; you benefit because now a woman in your workforce has had a positive experience with you as a leader and ally; and your organization is one step closer to a true culture of inclusion.

Listen, Really (A Reminder)

We covered listening from the head versus listening from the heart in the prior chapter, but it's worth pointing out the importance of listening from the heart, being curious, asking questions, and not defending or explaining. Rather than saying, "why didn't you call me?" Jerry could have made an empathic and accountable statement like, "I'm sorry you had that experience, it must have been difficult," and "Tell me more."

Intention Versus Impact

We know that being an ally and inclusive leader is a journey, and with it comes human mistakes along the way. It's what you do and say *after* your mistakes are brought to your attention that matters most. The core concept to learn is that it's the impact of your actions and words that you need to focus on and take accountability for, not the reasoning behind them.

Sharing your intention as to why you said or did something only results in the person who was impacted going unheard or unacknowledged, which is yet another impact. This breaks down the trust even further.

Every mistake you have ever made, you made with good intentions—are you willing to grant to others the same positive intent you grant to yourself?

Listening from the heart will improve your relationships, both personally and professionally.

TRAINING SECTION

I offer the following training exercises to support you in step three of the Ally's Journey. Typically, a microaggression you were responsible for will be brought to your attention by the person you impacted. The first training exercise is designed to support you in properly receiving feedback. The second exercise will help you have clean-up conversations. Lastly, there will be instances where these microaggressions didn't happen by your words, but from someone else on your team, under your leadership or supervision. This requires a different process.

Before we move on to exercises, let's review AFLA from chapter five, because it's applicable for this step of the Ally's Journey.

Accepting Feedback Like an Ally (AFLA)

1. Consider that the feedback given to you is supportive and can contribute to your growth. It took courage for someone to share that with you.
2. Be calm and find your center. Remember that this is their experience, that they have taken some risk to be vulnerable.
3. As you listen to the feedback, notice the feelings that come up inside you. Do you feel fear, shame, sadness, anger? Breathe and stay silent.

4. Notice if you want to defend, disagree, or offer an explanation. You are still in listening mode; stay silent. Focus on connecting to their experience and what happened to them.

5. Take a beat: Consider that the very thing you want to defend, disagree, or explain is perhaps the very thing you need to look at and get support around.

6. Say, "Thank You. I'm sorry, and I will work on this."

7. Honor your own process and proceed to the clean-up conversation model when ready.

CLEAN-UP CONVERSATIONS

Upon receiving feedback, clean-up conversations offer you an opportunity to get back in right relationship with another person who was impacted by your words and/or actions. This model can improve your ally and leadership skills and give you the ongoing confidence that, despite messing up (being human), you have a way to make amends and grow.

1. Ask the person who experienced your microaggression for an opportunity to clean things up.

2. Start by saying, "I heard what you said, and *I am sorry for the impact of my words or actions and how it made you feel.*" If they said your microaggression made them feel afraid or angry, include that in your statement to them. This validates their emotional experience and tells them you understand the impact.

3. Use restorative words: "My relationship with you is important to me and I'm committed to learning more about myself and how I interact with you and others."

4. Conclude with, "Thanks for listening to me, and is there anything you want me to hear?"

ORGANIZATIONAL ACCOUNTABILITY MUSCLE BUILDER

There will be instances where, as a leader, you learn of a variety of microaggressions that have impacted others in your division, on your team, or in your company at large. You will likely even witness a few of them. Creating psychological safety for women and marginalized folks is an important and necessary attribute of inclusive leadership. With this comes responsibility. You may not have been the transgressor, but you nonetheless have an opportunity to take accountability for what happened on your watch. This is a chance to establish what accountability looks like by bringing consequences into view so that everyone understands what behavior is acceptable and what isn't. This is a *two-part process*, the first of which is taking accountability for what happened.

Part One: Taking Accountability for What Happened

1. Ask yourself, "Did this occurrence happen on my watch?"

2. If yes, then ask, "What is my part in this that contributed to this occurrence?" This could be your lack of awareness, your silence, not setting expectations, and more.

3. Then ask, "Who or what is truly important to me, such that I would be willing to make a commitment to do/say something differently?" Presumably, it's the health and well-being of the individual, your team, and the culture of your company. It needs to be important enough to make a commitment to.

4. "What is my commitment to action?" This last step is the most important because the action you decide to take is designed to be the new behavior.

Part Two: Giving Feedback

Your responsibility as an inclusive leader will necessitate difficult conversations. There will be times when you need to bring to another man's attention the impact of his language or actions on another person. After you have run the accountability process on yourself, you are ready to give feedback to the transgressor.

1. Approach the individual and share that you have some feedback for them. Ask them if they are open to receiving it.

2. Emphasize that you are bringing them this feedback in support of them, and that it is part of your responsibility to create inclusive environments.

3. Make sure they are present to hear this; this cannot be done over email or phone.

4. Encourage them to resist defending, explaining, or mentioning that it wasn't their intent.

5. Share the data: "When you said this/did this . . ."

6. Share the impact: ". . . it landed on 'Michelle' as a microaggression"—e.g., she didn't feel included, it hurt her feelings, or she didn't feel supported. Let them

know that their focus needs to be on the other person's experience.

7. If necessary, share your own experiences of making these human mistakes.
8. Allow them a moment to take it in.
9. Ask them to share back to you what they heard.
10. If they are amenable, direct them to the clean-up conversation process.

CREATING SUPPORT—ESTABLISHING SUPPORT ACCOUNTABILITY

Being an ally and inclusionary leader is not something you can do alone. Resist the temptation to adhere to the man box rule that says, "Men don't ask for help." You need other people to stand for your success, and they need you. Of critical importance is understanding that your responsibility to learn falls on you and not on the oppressed person. Putting the burden of your learning on them is a no-no. Finding people like you—men, white people—to learn together and call out each other's blind spots is essential for your growth as an ally and leader.

Recommendation: Invite two men to form a small group that meets monthly. Use this opportunity to share learnings, current challenges, and questions you might have with each other. (I cover this in more detail in the Afterword, "Where You Go from Here.")

CONCLUSION

In this chapter's teachings of step three of the Ally's Journey, what is essential to point out is that as a result of step two—learning to truly listen with empathy and compassion—the stage has been set for you to move into some action. To move forward as an ally and inclusive leader, you learned how accountability, as a context, is necessary for you to be part of the solution of equity, inclusion, and belonging.

You learned about the importance of examining, owning, and using your white male privilege to support women and marginalized folks.

You learned how to receive feedback as a result of your own mistakes. AFLA, the process you learned in chapter five, was reintroduced.

You learned about organizational accountability and the importance of taking responsibility for what happens on your watch, as well as how to handle the unintended impacts of another's actions and how to give feedback to others with respect to their missteps.

You learned about intention versus impact, and how and why the focus should be on the impacted person's experience, not your or others' intentions.

In the following chapter, we'll look at more in-depth examples of errant behaviors driven by man box influences, and introduce some much-needed workarounds that align with healthy, inclusive masculinity.

Before you go, let's look at the key lessons you've learned.

> ❯ Key Lessons

Taking responsibility for your words, actions, and their consequences is true accountability and the mark of an ally and inclusive leader. By adopting this stance, you can be part of the solution of equity, inclusion, and belonging for everyone. Some key lessons to take with you are:

> As an ally and inclusionary leader embarking on your Ally's Journey, you will make mistakes along the way. What's most important is how you handle them.

> Accountability requires you to take responsibility— not just for words and actions, but for their impacts, intended or not.

> The only person who can hold you to account is you. It's your integrity that's on the line.

> Accountable leaders and allies take responsibility for what happens on their watch.

> When it comes to your mistakes (microaggressions), your intentions may be well-founded, but it's the impact and the experience of the other person that matters most.

< CHAPTER SEVEN >

STEP FOUR
OF THE ALLY'S JOURNEY

Think, Talk, and Act Like an Ally

THE MAN CARD

It's time to update your "man card." This is the score card that men all march to when it comes to being a man . . . at least, that is what has happened in the past. We all know how we have "kept score" on the man card before, from giving points for being "the tough, stoic, and emotionless guy," to taking points away for crying or not following the man box rules.

You've already learned about man box behaviors and how the old rules of masculinity don't serve anyone, including men.

With your new and developing understanding about what it means to be a man in the context of being an ally and inclusive leader, your old man card will be rendered invalid.

We will now be keeping score on our new man card (you can buy and use the Better Man Cards at bettermancards.com) to support your efforts. This is how we certify manhood, keeping score of what is and isn't perceived as manly.

< 141 >

It's time to update your man cards and align to your new insight to what it means to be a man—*one who values inclusivity and diversity and is an ally to those around us.*

This is where the rubber meets the road.

Up until this point, I've emphasized "doing the internal work" of being an ally. This next step is all about taking your internal transformation and using it to support full inclusivity—by thinking, talking, and acting like an ally. We will learn below about an organization that took this to heart.

This chapter is going to look and feel a bit different from the others.

I will show you some of the types of behavior that are typical for men in action, the impact and message they send to women, and helpful key tips that you can practice. We'll begin with the story of an organization that made the commitment to move its male leaders through a healthy masculinity training that supported them in updating their man cards—teaching them to think, talk, and act like allies.

Let's take a look at how one company decided to align their commitment to leverage its majority (men) with specific action to support their male leaders, update their man cards, and improve their score.

HEFORSHE IMPACT: PWC

Launched in 2015, the HeForShe IMPACT 10x10x10 is an initiative that convened ten heads of state, ten global CEOs, and ten university presidents to fast-track gender equality in world capitals, boardrooms, and classrooms.

HeForShe's IMPACT Champions came together in 2016 to share with the world the key obstacles they have faced on their journeys, as well as the innovative, proven practices that could now empower the rest of the world to create gender equality. One of those companies, PwC, has been a partner to my firm in various capacities over the last several years.

PwC planned to launch an innovative new curriculum to educate and engage men as gender equality advocates. It was their intention that, by learning and understanding the issues surrounding gender equality, men could actively make a difference and support women.

Chris Brassell, Director of U.S. Diversity, Inclusion and Talent Management at PwC, had spent much time and effort engaging and educating white male leaders inside his organization. A dear friend and colleague, Chris reached out to me and shared the firm's commitment with UN Women to sign up 80,000 men to join the HeForShe movement. Chris had been following my work in healthy masculinity and believed that the time was right to bring relevant content to PwC to support their men as allies and leaders.

Chris alerted me to the fact that Bob Moritz, Chairperson of PwC, had shared the story of how his organization went from 18 percent female representation in the Global Leadership Team in January 2016 to 47 percent by December 2016, twelve months later. It was now time to bring this effort into the rest of the organization.

Chris Brassell introduced me to Chris Crace, a leader at the firm and a veteran. Chris Crace participated on the panel at our New York Better Man Conference and vulnerably shared his challenges as a veteran and what it taught him about healthy masculinity; it was quite a touching moment that modeled for other men the power of vulnerability. Chris Crace then hired the Better Man Leadership team to create a four-part "healthy masculinity" webinar series to support their men to think, talk, and act like allies and inclusionary leaders.

We used our four-step Ally's Journey framework to support their male leaders, and we built four webinars to take them on a healthy masculinity journey. To support the men in "thinking like an ally," we introduced the following steps (which might just sound familiar).

For Step One: Acknowledge Your Stuff, we introduced bias, privilege, and outdated masculine norms for them to self-examine; more conscious ways of thinking, in spite of their biases; and the cognizance of their respective privileges and how best to use that privilege to advance women.

For Step Two: Listen, Really, we showcased the experience of others. Introducing empathetic listening built on step one, because we know, in our work, that empathy is the fuel for action.

For Step Three: Take Responsibility for being part of the solution, we introduced microaggressions and their impact, intention versus impact, and clean-up conversations. We stressed the importance of accountability.

Finally, for Step Four, the participants took the Better Man Pledge and made a variety of commitments to step into action.

A few months later, one of the leaders reached out to me via email and shared how he noticed, in a marketing campaign his team was about to launch for a pharmaceutical company, that one of their graphics included a picture of a woman nurse and a male doctor. He mentioned that this depiction was indicative of prior generations and not current times. This leader shared with me that he reached out to the team, shared his concern about the perpetuation of this male/female stereotype, and the team—which included women—supported his observation and changed the graphic to have a male nurse, and a doctor who was a woman of color.

Let's see how this male leader worked the Four Steps of the Ally's Journey:

1. **Step One "Acknowledge Your Stuff":** He attended the healthy masculinity workshop and raised his awareness of his and others' biases and privileges so that he could begin to recognize what they looked like in real time.

2. **Step Two "Listen, Really":** He listened to himself, thought about the experiences of and impact upon others viewing this graphic, and used his empathy as fuel to reach out to his team.

3. **Step Three "Take Responsibility":** Using his power, position, and privilege, he took responsibility for bringing his observation to his team's attention.

4. **Step Four "Think, Talk, and Act Like an Ally":** He shared with me his "new lens" on viewing all marketing materials and his commitment to bring to attention any indications of bias.

This was an example of real change that can occur after an organization and its individuals embarked on their journeys of allyship.

We're now ready to examine what it means to think, talk, and act like an ally and inclusive male leader. Some of this will feel like a review; I offer it simply to provide context of what you have unlearned, so you may now focus on what to do.

THINKING LIKE A (BETTER) ALLY

You can't think like a man if you don't know what old thinking needs to be abolished.

Thinking like a man requires introspection—becoming aware of our unexamined ways of behaving, which are often driven by unconscious thought. When we allow our biases to drive our behavior, microaggressions occur—instances of sexism, homophobia, racism, and more. They often manifest through language, errant gestures, or the way one looks at another person—behavior that affects people who belong to target groups. Microaggressions might also manifest as insults, derogatory comments, or gestures.

What is important to understand is this: Much of our programming as men and what it means to be a man, especially in relation to women, is from the past. What we saw modeled for us while growing up has been seeded deep within.

This is where the new man card score can change for the better! And it's exactly where you need to start—getting interested in what has historically driven your sense of being a man. It's why self-examination of our behavior is so important. This was some of the work you did in Step One of the Ally's Journey, Acknowledge Your Stuff.

Women and BIPOC know all too well what aggressive behaviors look, sound, and feel like. And unfortunately, they also know how these microaggressions, especially over time, limit their ability to bring their whole selves to work. It's time for men to get curious about the often-unconscious thinking that drives our behavior so that we can make adjustments that benefit all.

Let's go over the most common microaggressive behaviors and respective impacts I see in my work: manterrupting, misabropriating, and manopolizing. But remember that it's not only important to recognize them. *We must also change them during this last step in our Ally's Journey.*

Manterrupting

In Step Two of the Ally's Journey, "Listen, Really," I introduced you to the term *manterrupting* as an example of listening from the head. As you may recall, manterrupting is the unnecessary interruption of a woman by a man. According to a study from George Washington University that looked at business settings, including the Supreme Court, men interrupted 33 percent more often when they spoke with women than when they spoke with other men. *What is often hidden from us as men is that, on some level, we think it's okay to interrupt.*

Manterruptions often come from thinking that what we have to say is more important than what women or people of other groups are saying. Of course, that's just flat out untrue. We may have seen this modeled growing up and in the workplace; even worse, we may have been permitted to do it. However, its roots stem from patriarchy.

Let's refresh what we learned in chapter five:

> *When you interrupt a woman, it sends the message that what she has to say doesn't matter. When this happens repeatedly—which it will, until men break the pattern of behavior—women begin to change their behavior.*
>
> *The more you interrupt a woman, the less likely she will speak. The less a woman speaks, the less influence she is perceived to have. For her, this pattern typically translates to limited upward mobility and advancement. The company or organization misses her valuable input and contributions. Eventually, she leaves for a different position or organization.*

How to Change the Behavior: Key Tips

Amplify her ideas

You can break the cycle of manterrupting by amplifying her ideas, instead of breaking them down. This could look like saying, "I really like where you are going with this," or "That sounds great, can you tell me more?" This is really about encouraging her to step into her abilities and it also can bolster her confidence to bring her ideas forward more often.

Let her finish

For starters, let women finish speaking. When women share ideas, be curious and ask questions. Men often go straight to critical thinking—looking to point out the weak spot in any given idea. This undermines a woman's thinking. This is the impact we as men need to better understand "What happens when we do this?" It's important initially to allow a person, not just a woman, to have the opportunity to share an idea. Then you can ask if they are open to feedback. The failure to listen fully and evaluate a colleague's statements before offering critique is where the breakdown occurs. Women want their colleagues to respect their intelligence by giving them concrete feedback. They just don't want "straw man" feedback based on incomplete comprehension of their actual ideas.

Acknowledge her

Acknowledge her creativity by saying things like, "That was great, I want more of that!" You can also ask, "Have you considered . . .?" if you want to contribute in any way. This is more supportive language that will encourage her instead of knocking her and her ideas down.

Be fair and treat her like you want to be treated

Do you remember your first mentor? Imagine if they had busted your ideas down right out of the gate. By considering what she's saying and doing with a fair and open mind, and treating her like you want to be treated, you'll both win.

When you witness another man interrupting her

If you are a leader and you see a woman being manterrupted, your primary responsibility is to ensure that all voices in the room are heard. If you do nothing, your silence messages complicity.

Hint: It's wise to introduce a "no interrupting" rule in all of your meetings, and when necessary, to call out any inappropriate behavior. If you see it, simply lean in and say, "Hold on, let her finish speaking."

Extra-credit mentoring: It would also be a good idea to take the manterrupter aside, privately, and share with him why you intervened and what you've learned on this topic. While calling someone out for their behavior is sometimes necessary, a successful outcome depends on how you approach it. Men respond better to a one-on-one conversation, so a discussion privately will yield more favorable results than lecturing him in front of a group.

Note: You can refer back to chapter six, "Take Responsibility," and use the feedback model in the training session.

Misabropriation

Misabropriation, while not an official word in the dictionary, is a play on words that describes when a woman's credit for her idea is not recognized or when a man takes credit for it. This dynamic typically occurs in meetings that have far more men in attendance than women.

Let me give you an example of how this may show up in a real-world situation. A woman voices an idea in a meeting.

Following her idea, a few other people (usually men) chime in with input. Eventually, another man may share the same idea that the woman came up with first.

Misabropriation occurs when the men in the room give credit to the guy, even though it was the woman at the table who originally brought it up.

Impact: The message that this behavior sends to women is that their ideas don't matter, and that you and other men are not listening to them. It may also come across that you don't trust them or their contributions to the project or company. In this latter case, a woman will likely stop contributing her ideas and may start to look for a position elsewhere where her contributions will be considered. Additionally, you and the organization will lose out on her valuable ideas.

How to Change the Behavior: Key Tips

Give credit where credit is due

If it's her idea, keep it that way. Don't allow another man to take credit for a woman's idea. Effective allies encourage and support female colleagues to apply for next-level positions, speak up in meetings, and take the lead in certain situations.

When you witness another person misabropriating

If you are a leader observing someone misabropriating, intervene by reminding your male colleagues where the idea originated from. For example, you can say, "Hold on, Mike, Susan mentioned that a few moments ago." Make an effort to call on women and encourage them to contribute. Give her credit for her ideas and contributions in the moment in front of other men.

Manopolizing

The term *manopolizing* describes when a man verbally overpowers a woman or intrudes on her physical space during conversation, leaving little room for her to contribute. Simply put, it typically happens when men talk so much that they dominate the "air-space." While men have little to no problem jumping into or inserting themselves in a conversation, it may feel daunting for women to do the same, especially in a group of men. Women have shared with me that this is exhausting for them to do.

A quick story: My partner, Kriz Bell, is the only woman in a five-person partnership with myself and three other men. It was nothing short of exhausting for her to contribute her voice and participate in healthy disagreements with strong—albeit, awake—men who are "forever allies in training." The funny thing? My male partners and I weren't aware of her exhaustion until she told me. Once that door opened, we also learned that another female on our team was experiencing the same thing. So, what did we do? We made sure each man in the partnership became aware of this dynamic. Now, we designate one leader for each meeting, and we raise our hands (in front of the Zoom camera) to be called on by that leader. We put ourselves on mute until called. It's work—and it's working!

Impact: The message that *manopolizing* sends to women is that there is no room for their contribution. In this situation, there is again the danger that women will be silent, and everyone will lose out on their valuable contributions. Eventually, they may leave the company altogether.

How to Change the Behavior: Key Tips

Monitor yourself (and others)

First and foremost, monitor yourself. Ask yourself, "Am I dominating the airspace or am I allowing women in the room to contribute?" If you are leading the meeting, set intentions at the beginning of the meeting for everyone present to uphold shared airtime. You might even call attention to and educate men about manopolizing.

Educate without accusing

Be careful to educate without accusing anyone in particular of manopolizing. Otherwise, the men might shut down. You can call on and invite the contributions of women in the meeting from the start. This will communicate that you understand they deserve to be heard, and that those in the room want to hear them.

TALKING LIKE A (BETTER) ALLY

Talking like a better ally doesn't mean being aggressive, dominating, or belittling. Instead, it means being inclusive, patient, and unbiased. This requires, first and foremost, that we consciously think like an ally so we can communicate like one.

Let's review inappropriate language behaviors that typically show up in the workplace: sweet-talking, mansplaining, gender-biased vocabulary, and trash-talking.

Sweet-Talking/No Pet Names

Imagine you finish presenting at a meeting at work and your CEO says to you, "Nice job, babe." It's weird, right? Not surprisingly, women don't like being called pet names at the office.

New rule: If it's not her name, don't call her by it. While people of past generations may have thought communication like this was acceptable, it isn't now—and it probably wasn't okay with women then, either.

Impact: Sweet-talking sends the message that you don't see a woman as an equal, but instead, as an object. It confirms an unconscious power differential between you (the man) and them (the woman).

How to Change the Behavior: A Key Tip

This is simple. Use her name instead. It's time to completely lose the following words from your repertoire of communication with women in the workplace: honey, love, sweetie, babe, gorgeous, princess, kiddo, dear, and anything else along these lines. These terms of endearment may be very welcome with loved ones and friends, but to assume it's OK in the workplace with colleagues is a mistake.

Mansplaining

When men feel the need to explain something to a woman without her explicit request, it's called *mansplaining*. As a man, there seems to be something inside our brain that says, "I need to make this point clear." Sometimes we assume, from a point of superiority, that what is obvious to us as men isn't obvious to women.

Here is what this looks like in action—because I've done it! Imagine that in a group setting where there is a disproportionate number of men relative to women, someone introduces a concept. The mansplainer (a man) unconsciously assumes that the concept needs explaining to a woman in the room . . . because he believes she doesn't understand—and that is the misstep.

Impact: This type of explaining is condescending. Imagine if the roles were reversed and a woman went on a rant explaining something that you already had knowledge about. How would you feel? Would you form a judgment of her? Would you stop listening? Would you be insulted?

How to Change the Behavior: Key Tips

Work on noticing your desire to explain something

Ask yourself, why do I feel the need to explain this when I haven't been asked to do so? Since women have as much knowledge as men, you only need to offer your knowledge when you are asked to do so.

Notice others who mansplain

If you see this behavior happen in meetings or elsewhere in your workplace or organization, take a moment to evaluate. Did the woman ask for the explanation? If not, check in and ask her if any explanation was needed. Let her tell you. You can pull the man aside later and explain what you observed, why his behavior was inappropriate, and how it impacts women. Again, being a good ally means calling out behavior when you see it. Consult the Giving Feedback model in chapter six.

Gender-Biased Vocabulary and Communication

While calling a group of women "guys" might seem natural, it's definitely not right. And yes, I know women do this. But it's not okay for men to do. Additionally, being "girled" at work is just one way of subtly differentiating women from their male colleagues. Referring to an individual or a group as "girl" or "girls" is akin to making women seem more like kids and less mature than men. We don't hear people referring to "boys" in the same way that you hear the term "girls" used in the workplace—so just don't use it. I can imagine that your inner dialogue might think that this is overkill, but consider that in this instance, it's irrelevant what you think. *What is most important to understand here is how it makes women feel when you or other men talk.*

Impact: This type of language sends the message that you don't see women for who they are and that you are not inclusive. This type of vocabulary and communication excludes women from the conversation, and it's demeaning.

How to Change the Behavior: A Key Tip

Be more attentive to your language, and use gender-neutral language

When you start a meeting, for example, say something along the lines of, "Hi, everyone," or use another phrase that's inclusive. Don't use "Hey, guys." It's important to upgrade your language. Another way to be more inclusive is to raise your awareness of your use of the word "man." For example, instead of chairman, use chairperson. Instead of mailman, use mail person or mail carrier. There are many more examples, but these show how to change your vocabulary in beneficial ways.

In addition, avoid words that are derogatory and perceived as categorically feminine, such as: catty, bossy, hormonal, bitchy, and whiny.

Trash Talk

All trash talk is toxic. But derogatory talk about women, particularly at work, is absolutely unacceptable and propagates sexism. If you're not building women up, you're breaking them down. Most guys are very familiar with the type of trash talk that goes on in locker rooms. The language can be vulgar, foul-mouthed, and full of sexual references. This type of talk has no place in the work environment. It would be a mistake to assume that it's only women who get offended when they overhear these kinds of conversations at work; many men do, as well.

Impact: By allowing it to occur, you become part of the problem and won't be respected.

How to Change the Behavior: Key Tips

Stand by her, don't be a bystander

Healthy masculinity means building women up—so men must stop the trash talk.

Part of being an ally is not being a bystander. Stand by her, don't bystand her. Trash talk happens a lot at work and the only way it will stop is if you speak up. If you see someone else trash-talk, call them on it. Cut off these conversations as soon as they start. Check yourself and think about the women in your life. How would they feel if they heard you talk like that or, worse yet, stood silent while it happened?

Put on the cone of protection

If you are wondering what other guys might think of or say about you, consider this: What comes out of their mouth when you bring their language to their attention says a lot more about *them* than it does *you*. In fact, what they say has nothing to do with you. It is simply indicative of the unprocessed shame or embarrassment they might be feeling in the moment. Allow them to have that moment and don't respond. They will get the message.

Giving feedback to "that guy"

To be proactive, you can pull the trash-talker aside and say something like, "I'm not comfortable being part of this conversation. I invite you to consider that this type of talk is not you at your best." (You might need your cone of protection, in this moment.)

ACTING LIKE A (BETTER) MAN

Consider for a moment that the word *ally* is a verb. To be a true ally, you must "do" something. In all my years of inclusion work, I have repeatedly been asked the same question both by men and DEI professionals about the engagement of men as allies: "What do I do?" But it's not so simple as to tell men or their organizations just what to do.

That's because we, as men, need to examine what drives our thinking. Discovering the unconscious drivers of our thinking informs our language as well as our behavior.

When we begin to think more consciously as men, we can raise our awareness of our own biases and privileges—allowing us to make new choices that support new actions. Only then can we finally be congruent with our words, choices, and actions. Ultimately, it's our actions that will do the talking! Thinking and talking like a man without action is not enough. It's men using their power, position, and privilege to advance women and minorities that creates change that benefits everyone.

Acting like a man doesn't mean being the boss, working more hours, or expecting women to set up the meeting room and be the receptionist (in addition to the actual position she was hired to fill). It means having an equal share-and-care in your work environment. Here are a few ways you can take action.

Note-Taking

We all learned to take notes, whether it was in high school, college, or business school. It was one way to take responsibility and learn about any given topic. Historically, in the workplace, women occupied secretarial roles and therefore took notes at meetings. Unfortunately, women are often still associated with this role.

The (defunct) conventional thinking was that note-taking was a distraction and therefore a woman's task. This minimizes the woman's contribution and presupposes that she doesn't have much to contribute. It's sexist thinking; note-taking is everyone's job. It's up to men to correct this. Don't assume that women will take notes. Take your own notes. Better yet, offer to take notes in groups to model for some of the other men what it really means to "act like a man."

Office Housekeeping

Many offices have a communal kitchen. At home, most men are no strangers to doing dishes, emptying the dishwasher, wiping off counters, taking out the trash, and cleaning up after themselves. So why should it be different at work?

It shouldn't. Consider the motto, "Eat up, drink up, clean up." Pick up after yourself and don't leave chores for women to do.

Event-Planning

Holiday parties, birthday celebrations, and other important events at work require detail and logistical planning. These tasks historically fall on the shoulders of women. Next time there is an event to be planned, offer to take it on. Ask the women in your office for some mentoring, if you need it, but make sure you handle the actual work and implementation for the event.

Networking

Going out to lunch or drinks after work is a great way to build connections with other people and get to know them. As a leader, this is a great way to learn more about your team.

It's often the case that guys will congregate with guys. There's nothing inherently wrong with this. But when invites aren't extended to women, they miss out on the opportunity to connect and get to know other members of the team like the guys do. The result? Women feel left out. Additionally, any work-related conversation away from the office to which women team members aren't privy creates an unfair situation at the office.

Break down the boy's club divide and seek to be more inclusive, one invitation at a time.

> So far, we've learned on an individual level what it means to think, talk, and act like a man in the context of being an ally. We've identified where unhealthy masculine behaviors show up in the workplace, how they affect women, and some consequences of them. We have also learned behavior modifications that are more in alignment with being an ally and leader. But for true cultural change, organizations must be willing to embark on a multiyear journey and commit to a tried-and-true strategy.
>
> The next chapter will walk you through exactly how to implement a strategic process for your organization in order to gain true and lasting success based on inclusivity.

UPPER-DIVISION ALLYSHIP: ACTING LIKE AN ADVOCATE—PUSH, PROMOTE, PROTECT

There comes a time when an ally's small actions, while good and necessary, are not enough. For those of you in leadership positions, you may have heard of the term "sponsor." Maybe someone mentors you, or possibly you have mentored someone else.

The most well-known form of advocacy is mentorship. Data shows that people mentor people who are like them. Mentoring alone doesn't provide air cover or ongoing support and is not enough to push people past their comfort zone.

Rather than mentorship, the Better Man leadership team teaches a model of sponsorship. Advocacy means sponsorship which in action looks like: Push, Promote, Protect.

Push

Push means to encourage the person you are advocating for to go beyond their comfort zone. Women tend to be more discerning about applying for jobs, often wanting to wait until they have all of the qualifications to meet the job requirements.

If a job has five requirements, and a man has zero or one of the requirements, he often will apply. If a woman has four of the five, she will often tell you she is uncomfortable applying for it. As their sponsor, your job is to encourage them to apply.

In 2011, a special McKinsey Report produced exclusively for Women in the Economy: A Wall Street Task Force (created by the *Wall Street Journal*) found that one reason women hold back from applying is the presence of structural obstacles. The report's surveys and interviews found specific factors that hold women back or convince women that their odds of advancement may be better elsewhere. Women cited familiar factors that they find discouraging: lack of access to informal networks and lack of sponsors who can provide opportunities that male colleagues have.

Promote

By sponsoring a woman, you can promote female candidates—as well as their ideas—among male colleagues in your network, which is a great way to support the advancement of women. When you are in meetings or talking to a direct report or colleague, this is a great opportunity to share the success of the female candidates in your network.

Protect

As you have learned throughout this book, women and marginalized folks are impacted by the unconscious language and behaviors of others almost every day, if not every day.

As a sponsor, you can and should protect women and marginalized folks from men's sexist (and other "-ist") behaviors, as well as be on the lookout for unconsciously bias-driven decisions.

Imagine your company is hiring for a new role and considering a female candidate. If you hear a man assume that because she has a family, she won't accept the role if travel is required, you might bring that bias to his attention. You could say something like, "Let's not make that assumption for her; she's a great candidate, and we should let her decide for herself." As you learned in chapter one about man box behaviors, and as we discussed in chapter six: "Let her decide for herself."

A QUICK REVIEW OF
WHAT YOU'VE ACCOMPLISHED

You have successfully updated your man card! You may now consider yourself to be a man who values inclusion and diversity and is an ally to all of those around you.

You made the shift from doing the inner work of being an ally to stepping into thinking, talking, and acting like an ally.

You learned what mansplaining, misabropriating, manterrupting, and trash talk look like in the workplace, along with the impact these unchecked ways of being have on women. You learned about gender-neutral language and read several tips to counter these unconscious habits that men often exhibit.

In addition to learning to take initiative on several practical, day-to-day actions like note-taking, event-planning, running meetings with no-interruption rules, and more, you also learned about advocacy in the form of sponsorship using the three P's: Push, Promote, and Protect.

You are now equipped to start making daily changes to your behavior and language. With these key lessons under your belt, there is more work to be done to support organization-wide change so that more men like you join the movement of inclusion driven by healthy masculinity. In the next chapter, we are going to hear from a CEO of a large US-based company along with a Chief Diversity Officer who have made leveraging the majority a priority and enterprise-wide initiative.

< CHAPTER EIGHT >

THE MULTIYEAR GAME PLAN

For the better part of eight years, I have been encouraging organizations to engage their men in their diversity and inclusion efforts. It has never been easy. In fact, it was unpopular and largely not on the radar. Most companies, couched under the veil of "We don't want to exclude women," avoided explicitly focusing on their men.

I've knocked on the organizational door, invited men and their companies to the Better Man Conference, and worked with women in employee resource groups to partner with men to change the narrative. It has been a slow process. Few companies went all out; most dipped their toes in the water. Many passed on the idea.

Up till now, this book has been focused on how to become an effective male ally in the workforce. Most of what I have shared and guided you to consider is within your control as an individual. Ultimately, your success as a male ally and inclusionary leader in your company—for its culture to change to one of true inclusivity—requires a commitment from an organization to engage the

< 163 >

majority. An organization or company seeking to change must put intention and attention on men and the behavioral shifts that change will require.

In my work, I've also encountered a few organizations that understood the necessity of getting their men on board and were either doing something about it or were ready to explore what it would take to embark on a journey to engage their men in DEI efforts.

Engaging the majority is not a "one-and-done" process that can be accomplished by sending men to a Better Man Conference, or to any conference, for that matter. In putting more women and marginalized folks in leadership positions, broader representation in the boardroom, and true cultures of inclusion will require committing to a multiyear game plan.

Committing to a multiyear game plan to engage men is uncommon but necessary. Several companies are still looking at allyship broadly and not being overt when it comes to engaging the men in their organizations. And even more companies are unwilling to address systemic issues that occur as a result of unchecked patriarchy inside their companies. The companies that wait, avoid, and do not acknowledge the critical importance of including men will end up being the late comers—and that's okay.

I interviewed the CEO of a Fortune 20 company and the Chief Diversity Officer of a large financial institution, and I have shared their guidance, suggestions, and experience at the end of this chapter, which is preceded by my contextual roadmap.

Seven years into their journey led by Mike Kaufmann, Cardinal Health is the "Cadillac" model of male engagement. Moody's Corporation is an organization that is taking the engagement of their men seriously and has already made several steps in the right direction thanks to Chief Diversity Officer DK Bartley with the support of his CEO Rob Fauber, who has been on the Better Man stage.

This chapter is directed at those of you who are in organizational leadership positions: Diversity and Inclusion, Learning and Development, and HR professionals, or senior leaders who recognize the critical importance of engaging men as active participants in your company's commitment to a culture of belonging.

You might also be an *aspiring male ally* looking to make a difference at your company. You may want to have a better understanding of what's possible at an organizational level. In the Afterword, I share what you can do personally to sustain your education. I will also detail some steps you can take to get things going at your company if you are alone in this journey but see the institutional need.

THE ROADMAP: STEPS TO TAKE

ONE: Choose the context that supports your overall strategy to engage men— is it pain or possibility that is your motivator?

Most companies that are considering engaging men to become better allies fall somewhere on a pain/possibility continuum that informs their strategic efforts. On one side of the continuum is pain, and on the other, possibility.

Pain is when a company is in the spotlight for a leader's behavior that casts a negative light on the company and its culture. Other examples include when data reveals that women and marginalized folks are disproportionately underrepresented, with a pattern or trend of these folks leaving the company.

Companies that find themselves in this predicament can choose to react or respond. Like we heard in chapter one, the Hearst Corporation chose to respond when confronted with the behavior of one of its leaders. The pain was temporary. But it did send arguably necessary shockwaves throughout the organization, exposing a sentiment within its culture that Hearst wanted to correct. The possibility of creating a truly inclusive culture ultimately motivated them to embark on a journey to engage their men by sponsoring the Better Man Conference, sending a large cohort of men to attend, and holding a follow-up training for the organization's leaders.

Conversely, coming from a place of possibility allows companies to recognize the huge opportunity of leveraging the "over-represented" (that is, men) in current DEI initiatives. This will allow them to thrive, prosper, and emerge as "great places to work" where everyone can bring their full selves. A true sense of *belonging* felt by all, instead of only those in power, translates to the business success that so many companies seek.

TWO: Be overt as opposed to covert when it comes to putting attention and intention on the men in your organization.

Create an overall strategy to engage your majority as opposed to merely signaling that you will focus on men. I refer to this as putting intention and attention specifically on the men in your organization, from top to bottom. Many companies shy away from being specific about how they will train and coach men. Unless you focus on where the power resides and seek to dismantle unhealthy masculine drivers, you will perpetuate the very problem that you seek to remedy.

Recommendation: Specifically, this looks like male ally cohort trainings for men. The Better Man Leadership team offers a variety of engagement opportunities as well as cohort trainings.

THREE: There must be a recognition that this is a behavior-change endeavor.

If you want to drive sustainable change in your organization, it is men's behavior that needs focus and commitment. Men predominantly occupy leadership positions. Given that their behavior and language often negatively impact others and adversely affect business outcomes, the intentions of training, coaching, and conference attendance must include behavioral change.

FOUR: Conduct a qualitative assessment.

Whether you do a large-scale or small-scale assessment, being willing to actually learn about the experiences of the women inside your company with respect to the men is critical. When men learn of the experiences of women in their companies as a result of male behavior—without any shame or blame—it gets their attention and evokes empathy. Most men will then want to know, "What can I do?"

Recommendation: Conduct qualitative interviews with both men and women to ascertain their sentiments and the actual experiences of both genders, with respect to the company culture.

FIVE: Is senior male leadership ready to commit?

Unless senior male leaders are themselves learning and modeling ally-like behaviors, men in middle management won't have a model to follow and the microaggressive behaviors of men will continue. As a result, women and marginalized folks won't feel safe and won't engage fully.

Recommendation: Get a commitment from senior men, ideally in conjunction with the CEO, to receive ally training. Buy-in by senior leadership is a key component of engaging men; it can inform and support a company's overall DEI strategy. Conduct a modified training for these senior men. This will support subsequent efforts to engage managers, directors, and individual contributors.

SIX: Have a strategy to meet men where they are.

In chapter one, I introduced you to the five states of men in an organization. A successful strategy to engage men will require understanding how best to approach men in each state, so as to lead them to be part of a cultural change toward true inclusion.

I have listed the states of men below with suggestions of how to engage them.

> **Some men believe that their companies' DEI efforts threaten their jobs.**
>
> **Recommendation:** Introduce a training on privilege. It is critically important to *humanize* privilege for these men without a hint of shame. Supporting men in understanding their own privilege, and that with privilege comes responsibility as well as the opportunity to use it for good, is the initial approach with men in this state.
>
> Remember when you learned about privilege in chapter four, "Acknowledge Your Stuff"? This would be a good opportunity to share your own learning about your privileges, and your choices and intentions around how to use your privileges for good. In addition to having journaled several answers to questions about your privileges, I invited you to do an exercise around using the power of choice. Go back and see what you wrote and if it can support your role in a training for the other men to see and learn from.

Some men don't feel included in their companies' DEI efforts.

This is about both messaging and inclusivity. Relay to them that their contribution is important and needed. Invite them to participate.

Recommendation: Create a focus group with these men; seek their input and how they would like to be involved. Consider starting a men's ally ERG.

Lots of men are afraid to say or do the wrong thing, so they say/do nothing.

These men need both training and models to look up to. This is where the commitment of senior male leaders (mentioned above in point five) is critical to showcase their own commitment to move beyond being a bystander.

Recommendation: Start by conducting a town hall event or a conversation series with male leaders sharing what they've learned and how they overcome fears of saying or doing the wrong thing. Have senior leaders impart that mistakes are part of the journey and what's most important is how you respond responsibly when it happens. Send these men to the Better Man Conference.

Some men want to be part of the solution but don't know what to do/say.

These men are candidates to send to the Better Man Conference. They are also ready for training. These men will be your ambassadors.

Recommendation: Create a cohort of these men and send them to the Better Man Conference as a kickoff event that leads into a male ally training.

A few select men act like allies and already understand.

These men are your "plants" and should be considered valuable resources in your overall strategy. They don't need convincing; they need opportunities to lead and leverage what they know.

Recommendation: Incorporate them into your male ally training as examples of ally-like behaviors. Give them the opportunity to demonstrate vulnerability in town halls by telling their stories and learnings. Ask them to "grow the ranks" of men involved by inviting others along.

SEVEN: Provide a series of engagement opportunities for men to gain insight.

No one man is alike in terms of the way he learns. The light bulb might go on at a conference, while listening to a podcast, attending a training, or simply hearing another man share his story on a panel or at a town hall. The point here is that when committing to engaging men as allies, it's key to make available a variety of engagement opportunities.

Recommendation: Send your men to the Better Man Conference and other male-focused conferences (although there aren't many) or create a male ally "courageous conversation" series. This could look like a ninety-minute live or virtual panel where a few male senior leaders, along with a few women, explore the obstacles and opportunities of men being allies to women. You could collaborate with your ERGs to invite men to attend ally events, as well as trainings. There are books to learn from as well. I would recommend *Leadership 101 for White Men*, authored by my friend and colleague Chuck Shelton; *Why Women* by my friend and colleague Jeffery Halter; *Gender Intelligence* by Barbara Annis and Keith Merron; and *We're All in This Together* by Mike Robbins. Books that dive deeper into masculinity worth reading are *The Little #MeToo Book for Men* by my friend Mark Greene and *The Future of Men* by my friend Jack Myers.

EIGHT: Provide training and coaching.

Men who are willing to become better allies and leaders need training and coaching to sustain their learning.

Recommendation: Offer training immersions (both virtual and live), support individual and group learning, and use role-playing, instruction, and real business scenarios to anchor key concepts for men to use in their work environment. Coaching, both at the group and individual level, supports the deeper insights that certain leaders may not be able to get in training sessions.

NINE: Provide sustainable learning.

Successful behavioral change requires ongoing practice to maintain and ingrain the lessons men receive as a result of trainings, conference attendance, and coaching. When I did my men's weekend in 1999, I was encouraged to join a weekly men's group to incorporate what I learned and apply it to everyday situations as they came up—with the support of other men.

Recommendation: When considering a strategy to engage men, include a small group accountability program that follows a protocol small groups (of three to five members) can do on their own.

TEN: Include measurement as an imperative.

Participation: In starting an allies/leaders program for men, it's important that you first measure participation. It's critical that you agree on a certain set of activities. How many men are attending conferences, trainings, and internal events? Are you capturing feedback?

Representation: Do you have pay parity? Is your board diverse? What percent of SVP/EVP positions are held by women and people of color?

Having these goals in mind ahead of time serves as a context that will support your trainings and intended outcomes.

TWO LEADERS, TWO COMPANIES, TWO APPROACHES

Over the course of encouraging companies to actively target their men to be part of diversity and inclusion efforts, I have had the opportunity to meet a few good, courageous, visionary men in leadership positions. Below are the results of a conversation I had with two of these men.

These men have the courage, initiative, and heart required to lead the necessary effort to engage their men on a path of allyship and inclusionary leadership. One of these men, Mike Kaufmann, was ahead of his time when I had the opportunity to meet him and work with his male leaders in 2015. Mike is still actively involved in his company's diversity efforts, their primary focus now being racism.

Another one of these men, DK Bartley, wasted no time when we met in 2019 by being our host sponsor for our live NYC Better Man Conference.

Let's listen to what they each have to say.

Mike Kaufmann, CEO at Cardinal Health

When I met Mike Kaufmann in 2015, he was CFO of Cardinal Health. Rayona Sharpnack, CEO of the Institute for Women's Leadership, was working with Mike and his company and had just started to roll out male cohort trainings—something relatively unheard of at the time. Rayona and I partnered for a few years as Gender Allies.

Mike was integrally involved as an executive sponsor of the women's ERG at Cardinal Health, WIN, which stands for Women's Impact Network. An active sponsor, Mike attended meetings and drove robust discussions with the executive steering team and chapter leaders. He also spoke to all WIN members periodically.

In chapter two, we heard Mike's take on healthy masculinity and heart-based leadership. Below, our conversation continues; I was interested in both his perspective and experience as a male leader regarding what he had learned, what his advice might be for other CEOs, and his multiyear game plan for engaging men.

Mike's lessons along the way

When Mike first immersed himself in the work, his friends accused him of doing it to score points, but he didn't let it affect him. People initially questioned whether this was "flavor of the month" stuff—but because he kept talking about being a better man and ally, those comments rolled off his back. Some people were offended by the work Mike was doing, and a few mean comments flew his way (nothing really to speak of). Mike credits his willingness to be authentic as core to why people followed his leadership.

We talked about the importance of examining privilege. When I shared with Mike my strong preference to "humanize" privilege, he replied, "Humanizing privilege is super smart as opposed to criticizing it, because too many people assume the moment you talk about privilege, they will be criticized—and you know that nobody wants feedback around privilege." Mike then shared with me a male privilege questionnaire by NOMAS (the National Organization for Men Against Sexism) that poses forty-six statements to measure one's awareness about privilege. This survey is well worth it! Check it out at nomas.org/male-privilege-checklist and see for yourself.

On getting more men involved

Mike had some things to say about getting more men involved in inclusion efforts. He believes that it's critical to meet men where they are, without judgment, and to give them a chance to step up and try. It's also his belief that a lot of men find it difficult to surround themselves with people who are truth-tellers, which are essentially people who won't hold back the feedback you need to hear in order to grow as a leader. Mike took the time to seek out truthtellers. He offered that all men and leaders need to do this.

For Mike, receiving feedback is part of the journey.

Mike's offer to CEOs who are considering an "engaging-men" strategy

Mike offered unabashedly, "Don't start this if you are not really in, because your employees will sniff you out. You can't just write a check. . . . The authenticity is either going to come through or not." If you're not authentic, it's hard to get others to meaningfully change—because they are just changing out of fear.

When I asked him for specific advice that he would offer to CEOs when it comes to a strategy for engaging men, he said:

1. Don't do it unless you are serious.
2. Surround yourself with some truthtellers who you are willing to listen to.

3.   Be willing to educate yourself. Do the work.

4.   It's hard, it's forever, and you have to keep it up.

Mike is currently addressing racism in his company head-on. He has put himself on the learning curve as to how he can use his privileges to support his employees who are BIPOC. Mike shared with me his line of questioning when he talks to other CEOs about equity. He asks:

"Are you willing to understand the difference between equity and equality? If your answer is yes, do you know what that means? Are you willing to do more for your Black employees than your white employees? If you say, 'No, I'm not, because I am going to do this for everyone,' that's equality—not equity. If you aren't willing to take a step and do more, your employees don't trust you."

The distinction Mike points out between equity and equality in organizations (and in life) is important to note. Equity involves trying to understand and give people what they need to enjoy full, healthy lives. Equality, in contrast, aims to ensure that everyone gets the same things in order to enjoy full, healthy lives. Like equity, equality aims to promote fairness and justice, but it would only work if everyone started from the same place and needed the same things. As we know from learning about privilege, not everyone starts from the same place.

Multiyear game plan

When I asked Mike about his multiyear game plan, he mentioned his plan has two components:

1.   Agree on a certain set of activities and measure them: unconscious bias trainings, dedicated DEI town halls, specific cohort training for men, and inviting guest

speakers to allow men the opportunity to learn and have "aha" moments.

2. You have to measure representation. This includes pay equity, percent of women on boards, and percent of women in leadership positions.

Mike proudly shared Cardinal Health's current results: "We are at 99 percent pay parity with men to women. Our board is 50 percent diverse, and of eight direct reports, four are women, with one Black male." Of Mike's operating committee, the top eighteen is 50 percent diverse, and all four of the largest individual businesses are run by women.

In listening to Mike, what kept coming into my mind was that old Gatorade commercial: "I want to be like Mike!" All of us can seek to be our best version of ourselves, just like Mike.

DK Bartley, Chief Diversity Officer at Moody's

A diversity executive introduced me to DK in the summer of 2019, when I was looking for a host sponsor for the 2019 East Coast Better Man Conference in New York City. I was prepared to go into pitch mode, but in the first three minutes of our call, it became apparent to me that *DK was already on board*. DK was able to articulate to me the necessity of engaging men as part of his DEI strategy, unlike most CDOs I had encountered. This was refreshing!

The event was nothing short of amazing; Rob Fauber, now CEO of Moody's, delivered a heartfelt opening talk about his own healthy masculinity journey to being his best version of an inclusionary leader. DK recognized the importance of senior leaders being visible role models at the conference, and he made it happen.

Since then, DK (on behalf of Moody's) has gone on to become host sponsor for our International Men's Day event and also sponsored our UK/Western Europe Better Man Conference, for which he was a panel guest, in February 2021.

DK and I had a conversation about his approach to engaging men as a strategy and why it's important. He also had a few suggestions in support of other DEI leaders.

DK's take on healthy masculinity

When it comes to healthy masculinity, DK believes you can't differentiate between personal and professional. For men, it is really important to understand that we are the same guy both at home and work. DK posed the question, "Why wouldn't we practice healthy masculinity in both venues?"

Healthy masculinity in action, per DK, requires breaking out of old habits and moving forward to understand a better approach to gender that's not about where you come from. I took this as an aspirational intention that does two things: First, it brings awareness to old habits, and second, it offers a different way to see gender.

Lastly, DK took personal responsibility for his own healthy masculinity by sharing with me that there are three things he can do to be a healthy masculine man: "I can make myself aware, acceptable, and effective."

We moved on to guidance he might give male leaders. DK offered three points to consider:

1. **Take everything you know and throw it out the window.** This is about being open to learning new things instead of what you already know.
2. **Start to understand what a woman's experience is and what it means to be women in a world of men.** This is about seeking to understand that a woman's experience in both her personal life and at work is *very different than yours as a man.*

3. It's not about how you feel, it's how you make others feel.

This validates the concept of intent versus impact, which was covered in the third step of the Ally's Journey, in chapter six.

DK's take on heart-based leadership

I presented the heart-based leadership principles (emotional literacy, vulnerability, authenticity, accountability, inclusivity, and love), asking DK which, if any, figures into leadership that supports the engagement of men. DK immediately glommed on to love, saying that it is a word that is not normally used in a corporate setting. And conversely, when it is used, it fundamentally changes people's perspectives—in a good way.

He continued: "Part of the reason we partnered with Better Man is because we wanted to be able to talk to the men at Moody's [so] that they [would] view women at work the same way they view their daughters and partners. Many men equate love with wanting to protect and advocate. As a result, the conversation changes."

DK shared that he asked several men to use a portion of their budget to support pay equity; he reminded them that these women in the company are someone's daughter, someone's partner—effectively personalizing it. Many men at Moody's initially said, "We are not sure why you are making us participate but our motivation is, 'I have an opportunity to influence equal pay and it's my daughter or spouse [who] helps me relate.'"

Where DK Sees the Movement to Engage Men Going

It's a journey

DK emphasized the importance of walking the talk and acknowledging that change is not going to happen overnight.

It requires a commitment that is composed of a level of involvement, engagement, and sponsorship. DK went on to share that this journey will have *exponential benefits* that could result in greater revenue and/or a higher employee value proposition. To DK, you have to both recognize that it's a journey and understand that you are committing to being on the journey.

It can't be a start and stop.

It involves training

Part of engaging men to be part of a company's DEI efforts is learning and development. This includes understanding the relevance of external events, such as the nationwide protests for racial equality in 2020, and being able to explain/discuss what's going on internally at your company and how it applies to your leaders and your organization as a whole. With respect to sexism and racism, it's about educating. It needs to be acknowledged: "This is what's going on in the world and we need to understand how our clients, community, partners, and employees feel about this."

DK offered that this commitment will support breakthroughs over time. Astutely, he pointed out that a commitment to educate and engage your men allows you to mitigate future instances that could devastate your company, either financially or by exposure to reputational risk. DK insists, "We have to think about these things ahead of time."

Making an investment into the engagement of men

One question I had for DK had to do with the financial investment required and how to hold engaging men in the context of investment.

DK offered three tips:

1. Spend as much money as you can!
2. You have to start somewhere.
3. Look at what the data is telling you.

For those who are reluctant to spend, he suggested, "Resist the temptation to use lack of funds as an excuse. The very reason you're reluctant to spend is because you haven't seen the ROI [return on investment], which is over time."

What if I have a limited budget?

DK offered the following advice: You might not have the investment, but simply advertising this topic as important, especially when senior leadership is talking about it and supporting it, has value in and of itself. There are numerous avenues of low investment to commence your efforts. One of the least costly ways to get started is to send men to the Better Man Conference (without sponsoring). If you strategically pick a few leaders in various divisions, including sales, these men have the budgets to attend and will likely support subsequent efforts to engage men.

Why is sponsorship of conferences important?

According to DK, sponsorship is key. His opinion on sponsoring events is that it is the best way to sell an idea. It also allows you to see what new toys and bells and whistles are out there, just like in sales.

If you are going to focus on healthy masculinity, you need to go out and see what your competitors are doing. It's an opportunity to learn and understand what men are saying and how they are talking about it. DK encourages companies to "Get out of the bubble." You don't know what you don't know until you visit other locations. It allows you to see what your competitors are doing.

If you send the right people—or not the right people—upon their return, you will have a conversation about why or why not this is a great opportunity. Both of these conversations are beneficial. Lastly, you won't have the feedback if you don't participate.

DK's take on engaging men as a strategic imperative

I then asked DK for any guidance he might offer to his DEI colleagues regarding engaging men as a strategic imperative. If you are going to talk to a group of men—not just senior leaders but men coming into the organization—DK offered that you keep the following in mind:

1. **Speak to different ages (different voices).** The idea here is that men today are different than yesterday. Gen X, Millennials, and Gen Z all have had different experiences than those of the Baby Boomers.

2. **Understand, as a context, that DEI is innovation.** Engaging men in your DEI efforts can provide additional business opportunities. Think of it like an additional tool. If you don't understand women, that's a problem, because you can't relate. Understanding what to do and what *not to do* is even more important. Otherwise, you will miss out on opportunities. Any high-performance culture must engage the majority.

DK on measuring men's engagement

Our final topic had to do with measurement and metrics when it comes to engaging men.

DK offered the following: "Measure the conversations you are having."

> Are your men attending lunch and learns?
> Are they attending conferences?
> Are you implementing trainings?
> What has been the feedback?

There are several other companies with whom I have spoken, worked, and partnered, but very few have taken the steps to play the long game. Most companies elect to stick their toe in the water—or not get wet at all. My invitation for you is to consider: What game do you want to play—the long game (multiyear)? Or do you just want to dabble?

> ### ❯ Key Lessons
>
> I'm going to presume that you want to do more than dabble, so my intention here is to boil things down and give you the key lessons, in order.
>
> > ❯ **Engaging men must be part of DEI strategies.** The timing is NOW. More companies are open to focusing on engaging men than ever before.
> > ❯ **Focus on behavioral change.** Focusing on men's behavior as leaders and allies, without shame or blame, leads to culture change that can foster belonging and inclusion.
> > ❯ **Senior leadership must be committed and on board.** This is where the power resides, and along

with power comes the ability and responsibility to lead inclusively. The rest of the men in your organization stand to benefit from the modeling they see by senior male leaders.

> **Meet men where they are.** We've discussed the five states of men in your organization. Their states require slightly different approaches to be successfully engaged.

> **Commit to a series of "engagement opportunities."** Men experience insights in a variety of manners. Consider sending them to the Better Man Conference, conducting male allyship informative sessions (using senior leaders to lead), offering trainings and coaching, and more.

> **Commit to metrics.** This applies to both participation and representation. Once you agree on what engagement opportunities you will offer, measure participation in them.

> **Set goals.** When it comes to measuring representation, it's critical that you have intended outcomes in mind—including pay parity, percent of women on boards, and percent of women in leadership positions.

> **Invest the money.** For the very same reason you invest in talent development, spending money on the inclusive skill development for your men to become true allies and leaders will make your business thrive.

AFTERWORD

Where You Go from Here

I'M JUST ONE GUY—WHAT CAN I DO TO KEEP THINGS GOING?

I want to take this moment to acknowledge YOU for the work you have done thus far. The road to becoming an ally is not an easy one, but it is a rewarding one. You made the first decision to START. The next decision is to CONTINUE the work on yourself. The third decision is to ADVOCATE for the work in order to reach more men.

Showing up as a male in the workplace is now something you know how to do. You've put yourself on the path to becoming an ally and inclusionary leader. You've done the training exercises, you've reflected, you've learned. You are likely excited, motivated, and committed, and want to make sure you keep the momentum and don't revert to old patterns. You have a newer appreciation of what it means to be an ally and inclusionary leader. That's all good.

Maybe your organization is evolving and open to making this a priority, or maybe it isn't. Regardless, *you* are evolving, and you want to keep learning and being part of an important shift; don't let the lack of interest at your company stop you.

You might be an employee at a company that bought this book for you. Perhaps you're on a leadership team that suggested you read this. Or you might be running a small business and this book came on your radar.

If you have ever attended an inspirational conference or an experiential workshop, been impacted by a motivating keynote speaker, or read a good self-help book, you probably also had the experience of the post-event "return to the way it was" reality.

That's because these particular instances were not (and cannot) be designed to go beyond getting you to think, feel, and possibly make a commitment in the moment. Even what you may have learned in a self-help book, including this one, isn't worth much unless you apply what you have learned on a regular basis with practice. What happens after you go back to your company, community, and relationships is where the real work begins.

Continue the Work on Yourself

When I did my men's weekend in 1999, I was strongly encouraged to find, attend, and join a group of men that had previously done the same weekend I did. It was explained to me that the insights I gained about myself and new feelings would fade away over time and that I would likely revert to my old way of being, resuming the very behaviors I wanted to correct, if I didn't seek out support.

I recall at first having some resistance at the idea of committing once a week to spending a few hours with a bunch of guys I didn't know. But I decided to heed the advice, and I attended. In one night, I realized what it takes to sustain behavioral change. Doing my work as a man with other men, taking what we learned about ourselves as a result of our weekend experience and applying it regularly to life issues—that was the ticket!

I now refer to attending men's groups as metaphorically equivalent to regularly going to the "emotional gym," but in this instance, it's a gym that supports repetitions of awareness as well as building a partnership of the head and heart. This regular work has enabled me to stay conscious through life, and it still affords me a place to practice, receive support accountability from other men, and give my support to other men.

Putting yourself on the path to being a better man in your personal life and an ally and inclusive leader are one and the same. Neither can be done alone; both require a commitment to sustain your learnings. One avenue of continuing your work is to start your own "We" group, a small support group of three to five men. Below is an informal set of guidelines to get you started.

Start Your Own Ally Support Group

Start a small group (three to five men) of allies committed to meeting regularly. Use this framework:

> Check in with each other, one at a time. Name your pronouns, your biases and privileges that you know of, why you are here, and why this work is important to you. This check-in is for the first meeting. You can change up what you check in with to get things started.

> Share your current emotions in the moment (mad/sad/glad/fear/shame).

> Identify what specific behaviors you are currently bringing attention to and share any challenges you are facing currently. You may have actual work scenarios to share.

> ❯ Use this book and its exercises to drive your
> learning.

Lasting change, either for you personally or for your organization, requires a commitment. This commitment involves an appreciation of what true change requires. Behavioral change occurs over time.

In the introduction, I familiarized you with the five states of men inside your organization. Maybe you identified with one state at that time and now, at the end of the book, you find yourself in a different place with an expanded perspective. (I hope so.)

Up to this point, your journey has been purely personal. You've worked the steps, done the exercises, and learned how to think, talk, and act like an ally. Maybe you are even sponsoring a woman. That's great, and we need more men like you—a lot more! So, let's take a look at how you can grow the ranks of men.

STEPPING INTO ADVOCACY: MEN ENGAGING MEN

A Caveat

I remember when I did my men's weekend, one feeling I had was of joy, and it translated to me wanting all of my male friends to experience what I experienced. I came to realize that not all of my friends wanted to change or "wake up." They were either too afraid or too unconscious to realize that the issues they were having in life were the result of their way of being. The ones who were open and willing to self-examine and change their behavior did so; those who were not open or willing did not. A lot has changed over the last twenty years. Due to the COVID-19 pandemic and the Time's Up, Me Too, and Black Lives Matter movements, there is much more receptivity to change, especially in the corporate business environment.

Just know that although you are waking up to becoming an ally—and are now more aware of how you impact others and can empathize successfully with women and other marginalized folks—it doesn't guarantee receptivity from other men to step onto the path.

You will need to learn to meet other men where they are, devoid of judgment. This has been my experience for twenty-plus years.

Anthropologist Margaret Mead once said, "Never doubt that a small group of thoughtful, committed citizens can change the world. Indeed, it is the only thing that ever has."

I am enlisting you to support the overdue, much-needed Better Man Movement. Simply put, I need men like you to engage other men to be part of this. Make no mistake: This is a movement whose time is now, and regardless of your position, power, or privileges you can involve yourself and make a difference. It's time to become an advocate.

In 2018, at the Better Man Conference in San Francisco, we hosted a men-engaging-men panel with some male advocates. It was not surprising to learn that most men in leadership positions at their companies are engaged in the business, not in the business of engaging men. These advocates and leaders were needles in haystacks among thousands of unaware men focused on the business at hand.

I offer you to consider that to be a successful leader requires you to be part of DEI efforts and support initiatives to grow the ranks of men participating in the movement. You can start by simply recognizing that this endeavor is bigger than you and that you need other like-minded men alongside you. So, how can you make this a reality? Start a men's employee resource group to galvanize men to develop their allyship behaviors.

Starting a Men's Employee Resource Group (ERG)

There are several reasons to start a men's employee resource group, provided it is done under the right context. For starters, the model is proven and already in place for a variety of marginalized folks and their ERGs. If it can be a safe place for them, it can also be a safe space for men to start their journey.

Teva Pharmaceuticals, a client of Better Man Leadership, started their own men's ERG. They have attended the Better Man Conference and created a speaker series at which I have spoken and delivered workshops. This also resulted in a training for the senior leaders at Teva.

Cisco Systems, a sponsor on several occasions for the Better Man Conference, also started a men's ERG: Men for Inclusion (MFI).

Starting an ERG flies in the face of the man box rule that says, "Don't ask for help." It can be created as a forum to educate men who want to be educated, and overall, to galvanize men.

Some companies have a budget for this; many don't. Don't let that stop you. I will tell you what I have told many women who run employee resource groups and were interested in getting men involved as allies: *Find a male leader already on board, who has both the wallet and the understanding of the critical importance of engaging men in DEI efforts.* This male leader will be instrumental in making anything happen inside a company if he has position, power, and the courage to be part of the change.

Who can you invite?

Recall the five states of men inside organizations. Men in three of those states—men not feeling included in DEI, men wanting to be allies but not knowing what to do, and men who are already personally invested in the work—are perfect to invite to a men's ERG. Reach out to your DEI department and find out what it takes to get one started. If your company doesn't have a DEI department, then consult with your HR department. Be sure to be intersectional and include any and all men. Start by having conversations with men in your immediate business community, remembering to meet these men where they are.

A BOLDER CONSIDERATION

Summon your courage and conviction and survey your company to identify the one male senior leader who can appreciate and understand why engaging men in DEI efforts is important. Reach out to him and share your experience.

Share this book. If you have a vision like mine to make the world, including workplaces, a safer and more equitable and inclusive space, share it with another man and ask for his help. In my experience, most of the time it takes just one guy with position, power, and privilege to start the change effort. It requires courage.

And if this doesn't work, I invite you to give me a call! Change is not a matter of if—it's a matter of when.

ACKNOWLEDGMENTS

The women in my life

I could not have written this book without the help of strong, powerful, insightful women. There are women in my life who I have met along the way and deserve appropriate kudos for their positive influence on me in becoming an ally and inclusive leader. They taught me, they gave me the feedback I needed, they loved me for being the man I am. To me, that is true allyship.

First, my wife, Anna, who was there every day, encouraging me, nurturing me, and tolerating me during the whole process. Thank you, my love.

Second, Kriz Bell, my partner, my friend, my teacher. Thank you for not letting me slide and a big thank you for the title of this book!

Third, Rayona Sharpnack, founder of the Institute for Women's Leadership, who gave me my start on this journey. Thanks for believing in men and taking the risk of bringing me on.

Fourth, Nancy Shanteau, my coach, for helping me get the book started; thank you for believing in me and reminding me of what's truly important.

Fifth, my agent and advocate, Michele Martin, who guided me through the process of aligning with the right publishing company, Diversion Books. Thanks for your persistence and sharing my vision.

Sixth, my new friend Emily from the Diversion Books team, who made the editing process a collaborative, energizing, and memorable experience.

My mom, Elaine, my daughter, Emma, and my sister, Sandy, thank you for being the feminine familial influence that motivates me to do this work.

《 》

The men in my life

In twenty-two years of men's work there have been many men who have positively influenced me, for which I am grateful. Special thanks to the ManKind Project for their role in supporting me to be the man and leader that I am today.

There are a handful of men that I wish to acknowledge for their role in making this book a reality.

Thanks to my partners, Ed Gurowitz, Jon Levit, and Robert Beaven, for holding me accountable, giving me feedback, and loving me along the way.

My dear friend and men's group buddy, Mike Robbins, for hooking me up with my agent and sharing your process as a published author to get me going.

Dad, you showed me what it means to be a true civil servant and I want to thank you for being such a great role model!

Keith Wallman, editor in chief at my publisher, thanks for believing in me, partnering and joining the movement, and using your platform to advance the message.

《　》

And last but not least, thank you to God for blessing me with the opportunity to write this book.

SELECTED REFERENCES

Annis, Barbara and Keith Merron. *Gender Intelligence: Breakthrough Strategies for Increasing Diversity and Improving Your Bottom Line.* New York, New York: Harperbusiness, 2014.

Bettermanconference.com.

Bodie, Graham D. "The Active-Empathic Listening Scale (AELS): Conceptualization and Evidence of Validity within the Interpersonal Domain." *Communication Quarterly* 59, no. 3 (2011): 278.

Bodie, Graham D. and William A. Villaume. "Aspects of Receiving Information: The Relationships between Listening Preferences, Communication Apprehension, Receiver Apprehension, and Communicator Style." *International Journal of Listening* 17, no. 1 (2003): 48.

Bruneau, Tom. "Empathy and Listening." *Perspectives on Listening*, eds. Andrew D. Wolvin and Carolyn Gwynn Coakley. Norwood, NJ: Alex Publishing Corporation, 1993. 188.

Connley, Courtney. "A year ago, women outnumbered men in the U.S. workforce, now they account for 100% of jobs lost in December." *CNBC: Make It.* January 11, 2021.

Coury, Sarah, Jess Huang, Ankur Kumar, Sara Prince, Alexis Krivkovich, and Lareina Yee. "Women in the Workplace 2020." *McKinsey and Company.* September 30, 2020.

Greene, Mark. *The Little #MeToo Book for Men.* Thinkplay Partners, 2018.

Halter, Jeffery. *Why Women: The Leadership Imperative to Advancing Women and Engaging Men.* Fushian, 2015.

Hargie, Owen. *Skilled Interpersonal Interaction: Research, Theory, and Practice.* London: Routledge, 2011. 205.

Kivel, Paul. "Act Like a Man Box." paulkivel.com/wp-content/uploads/2011/09/actlikeamanbox.pdf. 2007.

Kivel, Paul. *Men's Work: How to Stop the Violence That Tears Our Lives Apart.* New York, New York: Ballantine Books, 1995.

Milardo, Robert M. and Heather Helms-Erikson. "Network Overlap and Third-Party Influence in Close Relationships." *Close Relationships: A Sourcebook*, eds. Clyde Hendrick and Susan S. Hendrick. Thousand Oaks, CA: Sage, 2000. 37.

Myers, Jack. *The Future of Men: Men on Trial.* Inkshares, 2016. Rayarata.com.

Robbins, Mike. *We're All in This Together: Creating a Team Culture of High Performance, Trust, and Belonging.* New York, New York: Hay House Business, 2020.

Shelton, Chuck. *Leadership 101 for White Men: How to Work Successfully with Black Colleagues and Customers.* Morgan James Publishing, 2008.

INDEX

ABOUT THE AUTHOR

Ray Arata is an award-winning leader in the field of diversity, equity, and inclusion (DEI), specifically known for his work in engaging men as allies. In addition to amassing more than 13,000 hours leading workshops for men, Ray is the founder of the Better Man Conference. He is a sought-after speaker, consultant, and trainer, delivering keynotes and facilitating trainings for massive global clients such as PwC, Toyota, Genentech, Verizon, Bloomberg, and many more.

Ray's Better Man Conference, as seen in *Forbes*, *The Good Men Project*, and *Fortune*, is an international industry-leading event that focuses on the development of healthy masculinity and men as allies and partners. Prior to the pandemic, the conference was held in New York City and San Francisco, drawing almost two hundred major organizations annually. Under Ray's leadership, the conference has attracted an impressive list of sponsors, including Hearst, Moody's, CBS, Toyota, Intel, HP, Cisco Systems, the *New York Times*, and others.

Ray was recognized in 2016 as a HeForShe Champion for Change, awarded by UN Women, and honored with the Ron Herring 2020 award (originally named for the ManKind Project, a global network of charitable foundations). His first book, *Wake Up, Man Up, Step Up: Transforming Your Wake-Up Call to Emotional Health and Happiness*, was published in 2013 by Highpoint Publishing.

Ray lives in Fairfax, California. For more information on his work, visit rayarata.com and bettermanconference.com.